Care and Maintenance
of the
Christian Life

William L. Blevins

Mossy Creek PRESS

CARSON-NEWMAN COLLEGE

Care and Maintenance
of the
Christian Life

William L. Blevins

Mossy Creek Press

To order additional copies of this book, contact:
Mossy Creek Press
1-423-475-7308
www.mossycreekpress.com

This book is dedicated to my wife and kids
and especially to my grandkids
Alex, Jaclyn, Sydney, Noah, Neal

CONTENTS

Preface

As a Christian, what do you do when the euphoria of your conversion experience wears off? How do you respond to God when you realize that faith in Jesus does not automatically solve all of your problems and answer all of your questions about life? What can you do when your life gets back into the same old rut?

This book is my attempt to answer briefly one question: "What does a Christian need to know to adequately begin his spiritual pilgrimage?" My simple answer is that he needs to understand some basics about what salvation is about. He needs to have a mental grasp of what he has experienced with God. And beyond that, the Christian needs to develop some basic skills that facilitate growth and maturity in the faith.

Oliver Wendell Holmes once said that it is not so important where a person stands as the direction in which he is moving. This book is intended to help Christians move in the right direction in their relationship with God. It is designed to enable the reader to press forward to God's upward calling.

Many of my friends and colleagues have given help and encouragement to me as I completed this book, I owe each of them my deepest gratitude.

WILLIAM L. BLEVINS

Introduction

WELCOME TO THE JOURNEY

Real is how you are made. It's a thing that happens to you. When a child loves you for a long, long time, not just to play with, but REALLY loves you, then you become Real. It doesn't happen all at once. You become. It takes a long time. Generally, by the time you are Real, most of your hair has been loved off, and your eyes drop out and you get loose in the joints and very shabby. But these things don't matter at all, because once you're Real you can't be ugly, except to people who don't understand.

-Margery Williams
The Velveteen Rabbit

ARE YOU A REAL PERSON? Are you fully alive? Realness-being all that you can be--is not a quality everyone possesses. It must be discovered. A person must become

9

real. It does not happen automatically. Are you real? Or do you know deep in your bones you're a phony? The Christian faith helps you to become a real person.

If you are a new Christian, this book is written especially for you, but not exclusively for you. "Old timers" in the faith might also find it helpful, for it is written to answer two basic questions about the Christian faith: What is salvation? What am I to do now that I am saved? Those of us who have been in the church for a while expend considerable energy telling people how to get saved. Yet sometimes we do not give adequate attention to teaching new converts how to be saved. And that is very important. As a new Christian you have some spiritual growing up to do. We all do. Even the Apostle Paul confessed late in his ministry: "Brethren, I do not regard myself as having laid hold of it yet; but one thing I do: forgetting what lies behind and reaching forward to what lies ahead. I press on toward the goal for the prize of the upward call of God in Christ Jesus" (Phil. 3:13-14, NAS). After more than thirty years in God's service, Paul had not arrived; he was not fully what God wanted him to be. Yet we still call him Saint Paul. He was a "becomer."

Keith Miller[1] defines a "becomer" as a convert who has been freed by Christ to begin actualizing the potentialities inherent in his life from birth. A "becomer" is a person-in-process. A "becomer" is a person who is bringing into being all that he can and ought to be. A "becomer" is one who dares to do God's will in his own life. And now that you have committed yourself to Jesus, you too are a "becomer." God has started a process in your life to liberate all your latent abilities and potentialities. He is creating in you a person who is fully alive and real. You are already on your way to becoming someone who today is wonderfully different from the person you were yesterday. The New Testament has spoken about what has started happening in your life: "As many as received Him, to them He gave the right to *become* children of God, even to those who believe in His name" (John 1:12, italics mine). God has started fashioning you into the image of his son (Rom. 8:29). You are becoming the person he wants you to be.

Off on the Right Foot

Our world is filled with people who value good beginnings. We are told that good beginnings are important. We are influenced in many subtle ways by this "right foot" philosophy. How often has someone encouraged you to get off on the right foot? The situations may vary, but the admonition remains the same. It may be the start of a new school year, the first day on a new job, the initial stages of a friendship, or even the beginning of a marriage. The implication is that getting off on the right foot is the most important facet of any experience. We seem to be enchanted by the magic of good beginnings.

Good beginnings are important. And they are as important in salvation as in any other area. You have experienced many beginnings in your life. And now you have accepted the challenge of another one. You have begun a pilgrimage with Jesus. You have been "made alive" in Christ (Eph. 2:5). You have chosen to walk the life road. This new beginning is most important for you as a person. It will change the entire shape of your being. In choosing to follow Jesus, you are getting off on the right foot with your own life and with God.

And a Good Ending Too

A good beginning in salvation is absolutely necessary to experience the abundant life that Jesus offers you. But it is not enough by itself. A good beginning is not the most important aspect of experience. A good ending is just as vital. The salvation process already begun in you needs to be brought to completion. This is why Jesus taught that discipleship involves more than an enthusiastic beginning. His parables about the king going to war (Luke 14:31-33) and the farmer constructing a building (Luke 14:28-29) teach that one should not even begin the salvation journey if he is not prepared to finish it. And this is why Jesus said that a person who puts his hand to the plow and looks back is not a worthy disciple. It is as important for you to end up on the right foot with God as it is to get off on one.

Your recent spiritual birth was the most dramatic beginning of your life. Yet it was only a beginning. God has much more in store for you. In all of your daily experiences— the ups and downs, joys and sorrows, laughter and tears, failures and successes— there will be a new you becoming every day. You can depend on it. And if you focus closely upon your life, you will discover "old" things passing away and all things becoming "new" (2 Cor. 5:17). God is already working in all of your experiences for your good (Rom. 8:28). God has started a new work in you, but he is not yet finished with you. Your conversion is a beginning, not an arrival. It is a pilgrimage, not a position. And you may be assured that God wants to bring your salvation to completion: "For I am confident of this very thing, that He who began a good work in you will perfect it until the day of Christ Jesus" (Phil. 1:6, NAS).

Just for You

Becoming a Christian means putting the world into different focus. Few things are going to remain the same for you, or even look the same. And it's not going to be easy. Your faith will demand new responses to friends and family. You will eventually struggle with doubt and temptation. It will sometimes be difficult to put your finger on the right thing to do. There will be those inevitable hours when you feel alone and abandoned by everyone. You will wonder if life has any real meaning at all. And there will be those peak experiences when you will walk on the mountaintops. The point of all this is that God is not going to drop the abundant life in your lap. You will discover it as you share the journey with Jesus. You will possess the abundant life as you grow and cope and mature. But how do you do that? You have become a Christian by committing yourself to Jesus, but where do you go from here? What is the next step?

This book is written for Christians like yourself. The following chapters contain some basic information that every new Christian needs to know. The book is intended to help you get off on the right foot in your relationship with God. And it offers some guidelines to facilitate your spiritual growth. Some of the chapters will help you better understand what has happened to you in your salvation experience and how you can become real. In a word, this book will point you in the direction of being a faithful "becomer."

I will write informally in the following pages and will address you personally. And I want you to know at the outset that I am not an expert Christian. I do not have all the answers about life or the Christian faith. I don't even know all the questions! Nor has God completed his work in me. I am still a "becomer." I address you merely as a fellow pilgrim on the life road. I share with you a deep commitment to Jesus Christ. And I share other things with you as well. I yearn to grow out of my phoniness and become a real person. I struggle with life as you do. Sometimes I hurt inside. There are times when my inside hurts are as painful as any physical discomfort I have ever experienced. There are times I have difficulty getting it altogether. My life frequently unravels a bit and at times my little ball of wax begins to melt. God does not immunize any of us against life. But neither does he abandon us to life. I have discovered that faith in Jesus enables me to cope with life and grow in the process. The same resources for coping and growing—for becoming—are available for you. Yet growing in the faith doesn't happen automatically. The Christian life cannot be "played by ear" like a piano. We must take up Christ's yoke and learn how to follow him (Matt. 11:29). Only then can we become real, authentic disciples. Toward that end, I am reaching out to you in the following pages. You have committed yourself to Jesus. You are a fellow pilgrim. Welcome to the journey. Take it from me, it's worth the trip!

Part One

When I was in college, it was fashionable for societies to initiate new members by blindfolding them and dropping them somewhere in the boondocks. The initiates then had to find their own way back home. But first they had to figure out where they were. Only then could they get to where they wanted to be.

Have you ever used a road map? The first thing you do is locate where you are. Then you find where you want to go and figure out the best route from one to the other. To get anywhere in life you must first find out where you are. All your journeys begin there. And this is especially true of your spiritual pilgrimage. You have begun the journey with Jesus, but you have not yet arrived where God wants you to be. This book is intended to help you on your journey. The first section is designed to assist you in locating where you are spiritually. It is written to deepen your understanding of what salvation is and how you have experienced it. Only when you understand where you are spiritually can you realistically get on the move to where God wants you to be. You will notice that I have written in such a way as to involve you in Bible study. That book alone will be a "light for your path" the entire journey.

1

SPEAKING IN PICTURES

THE IMAGE IS VIVIDLY ETCHED in my memory. My nine-year-old daughter and I were on the road– I in the driver's seat, she kneeling in the back with her elbows on the front seat and her chin resting in her hands. It was common for her in those days; from this semi-prayerful position she would talk as we drove down the highway.

On this particular occasion I had just picked her up from a summer church camp. "Dad," she said matter-of-factly, "One of the counselors talked to me yesterday about becoming a Christian. She read to me out of the Bible and said Jesus would come into my heart if I asked him. So we got on our knees and prayed."

A feeling of joy began to surge within me, but years of practice as both minister and counselor had me stuck in a role-rut. In my most professional counselor tone, I asked,

"And what did you say in your prayers?"

"I asked Jesus to come into my heart," she stated simply.

I paused a moment, wanting her to take the initiative in answering the next obvious question. When she made no visible effort in this direction, I put it to words. "Suzanne, did he come into your heart?"

She paused, cocked her head to one side and looked at me incredulously. "Well, how would I know?"

We drove in silence.

One year later it was almost rerun time, but not quite. Suzanne was coming home from camp with some friends. I was standing in our breakfast nook with a cup of coffee in one hand, trying to force the world awake. All of a sudden and with one flash of excitement, Suzanne came bounding through the nearest door. "Guess what?" she shouted at the top of her voice. She answered her own question before I could venture a guess. "I became a Christian this morning," she beamed. I shared her joy and enthusiasm. We sat at the table and talked about it. She related the whole experience and a part of the conversation went something like this:

"My counselor invited us to accept Jesus as savior and I did." "Did what?"

"Accepted Jesus."

"I know. But what does that mean to you?"

"I let him come into my heart."

"I know. But what does that mean?"

"I let him sit on the throne of my life."

"I know. But what does that mean.,"

"He's going to be the ruler of my life."

"I know. But what does that mean?"

In total frustration at not being able to communicate her experience to her father, she responded with a degree of finality, "It means, Dad, that I'm going to obey Jesus from now on. I'm going to live the way he wants me to."

Bingo!

It was obvious to me that she was answering my litany of questions with phrases she picked up at church and camp—" accepted Jesus," "let him into my heart," "put him on the throne of my life." She had the terminology mastered, but did she know what it meant? Could she put her finger on her own feelings and experience? She removed all my doubts with that last-ditch, theologically stripped-down affirmation. Obeying Jesus. Behaving the way he wants. That's about as down-to-earth and realistic a description of salvation as any child can grasp.

The Necessity of Picture Talk

Have you noticed that we talk in pictures when referring to our experiences with Jesus? Like my daughter, we use metaphors to describe salvation. And we have an almost inexhaustible supply:

"I've been born again."

"I am saved."

"Jesus lives in my heart."

"I've met the Lord."

"I've seen the light."

"I've got religion."

We talk in pictures about salvation because that's the only way we can talk about it. Salvation is an experience that touches every dimension of your being. It is a process that changes you from the inside out and involves the way you feel, think, behave, and relate to others. It influences your values, goals, and purposes for living. It affects your self-concept, body image, and whole psychic structure. Our language is simply inadequate to directly express an experience of this magnitude. We cannot talk it literally, so we talk about it. We use pictures to describe what salvation is like.

The Nature of Picture Talk

You can better understand the Bible if you are tuned into the nature of its language. And the Bible uses many metaphors to describe salvation. For this reason, you should know several things about the nature of metaphors in order to get in touch with both the biblical message and your own experience.

First, *it is normal for you to use metaphors when speaking about religious experiences.* You talk in pictures every day. These pictures, or metaphors, clearly communicate what you are trying to say, and you intuitively understand their meaning. In the course of a normal day, you can get packed into an elevator like a sardine, level with a friend about a problem that's been bugging you, or do a slow burn because some nut pulled the wool over your eyes. You can turn green with envy over a neighbor's new car or get caught in a traffic bottleneck in your own. You can become flushed with embarrassment at the drop of a hat and get down in the dumps when your plans fall through.

Your everyday speech is laced with metaphors. That's normal. And it is no different when you talk religion. The writer of Hebrews, for example, spoke of the Christian life as a race: "Therefore, since we are surrounded by so great a cloud of witnesses, let us also lay aside every weight, and sin which clings so closely, and let us run with perseverance the race that is set before us" (Heb. 12:1). Paul described our spiritual pilgrimage as a battle: "Put on the whole armor of God, that you may be able to stand against the wiles of the devil" (Eph. 6:11). He also likened his service to God to that of a farmer: "I planted, Apollos watered, but God gave the growth" (1 Cor. 3:6). He considered his work to be like that of a builder: "According to the grace of God given to me, like a skilled master builder I laid a foundation, and another man is building upon it. Let each man take care how he builds upon it" (1 Cor. 3:10). And Simon Peter sounded like a pediatrician when he pictured salvation: "Like newborn babes, long for the pure spiritual milk, that by it you may grow up to salvation" (1 Pet 2:2-3). It is almost impossible to talk religion without using picture language.

Wallace Hamilton tells the story of a mother who was gripped with concern for her young son during a thunderstorm. She ran upstairs expecting the child to be terrified and was fully prepared to alleviate his anxiety. But she was not prepared for what she saw when she opened his bedroom door. The boy was excitedly looking out the window at the storm. With every clap of thunder he yelled, "Bang it again, God. Bang it again!" We use a lot of pictures when we talk about God and religion. And you will find that the Bible also is filled with religious metaphors. The people God inspired to write the Bible spoke in pictures too.

Second, *metaphors are stand-ins for reality*. You use metaphors in your everyday speech without giving them a second thought, and you clearly grasp their meaning. But you do not take the metaphors literally. You know quite well that metaphors are merely pictures for realities. Envy does not literally cause you to turn green. Someone does not have to literally touch you to pull your leg. And Mondays are not really blue. Metaphors just stand in for realities.

This is also true of religious metaphors. Our language is totally inadequate to speak directly of ultimate reality, so we use familiar images to describe what it is like. We use common everyday words to express something of the wonders that lie beyond the observable world. We use the temporal as an idiom for the eternal. Thus, we might describe God as a judge, or a father, or a king, or a shepherd, or a potter. We might speak of Jesus as the lamb of God, the water of life, the light of the world, or the bread of heaven. Yet we know that God is not a literal shepherd any more than we are actual sheep. And Jesus is not literal bread or water. All such metaphors describe realities, but are not themselves the realities they describe. They only picture what reality is like. They are signposts that point beyond themselves.

Take the biblical metaphors seriously. Discover the truths they portray. But don't take them literally. A person who confuses a metaphor with the reality it represents is like a person who goes into a restaurant and eats the menu. The words on the menu point beyond themselves to the real food that can satisfy your hunger. The menu-words themselves are not very nourishing. And that's the way it is with picture language. Metaphors are stand-ins for realities.

Third, *the biblical metaphors for salvation are practical in nature.* The men who wrote the Bible were not trained theologians. They were all persons much like yourself who experienced God in their own lives. God inspired them to write from their experiences in practical, down-to-earth images. Jesus himself talked in pictures when he spoke about salvation. Paul used practical images too. So did the early church. And so do those of us in the church today. We echo the picture-talk of our first-century brothers.

Yet there is one difference. In the nearly two-thousand-year interval between their time and ours, the practical images used by the New Testament writers have become theological ones for us. We speak of Jesus as living water, but we don't think of water as the precious commodity it was in the Middle East of Bible times. We get water from a faucet. Or we say, "The Lord is my shepherd." Yet most of us, if we live in a city, go for years without ever seeing a sheep. The writer of the Psalm lived every day with the practical issues of tending sheep.

The metaphors the early Christians used were picked because they were vivid pictures—they caught the fancy and sparked the imagination of the people in the first century. These metaphors can have the same magic for you today when you dig through the layers of theological crust to recover their practical meanings.

Fourth, *each salvation metaphor pinpoints a real human experience.* The Bible is a book about people—real people like yourself. People who cried and laughed. People who worked and played. People who hurt and rejoiced. People who were both good and bad at the same time. People who succeeded and failed. People who fought and lived in peace. People who were disillusioned and yet clung to hope. People who loved and hated. People who gave birth and died. People who struggled with life. And people who encountered God and lived to tell about it. Their experiences with God shaped their ideas about God and life and salvation. But the metaphors they used were not intended simply to communicate ideas. The biblical writers wanted to communicate their experience with God. That's one reason they used so many different metaphors. No single metaphor could express the complete experience any more than one piece of a puzzle discloses the whole picture.

They used numerous metaphors as pointers to what salvation is like when a person experiences it for himself.

Theological Terms

Our religious vocabulary is crowded with some big words—*Salvation. Justification. Reconciliation. Sanctification. Regeneration, Redemption. Atonement.* Words like these are not exactly metaphors, but we have some of the same problems with them that we have with biblical picture-talk. Words like these are not practical tools for us. Most of us stumble over their meaning. They are seldom used outside the church. They are not what you would call turn-on words for our generation. And they probably don't strike very much fire in your bones unless you are interested in studying theology. Yet this was not the case for the early Christians.

These words—or at least the words they are translated from—were based on common terms. Christians borrowed the words they used from everyday life. Their vocabulary was the vocabulary of the real world where people lived and breathed. The same words that sound like some unknown tongue to us were charged with meaning for people in the first century.

So when you bump into these big words, or into the salvation metaphors used in the Bible, look for the experience that hides behind the picture. Use biblical metaphors to probe your own inner space. How do theological words like sanctification and redemption enlighten your understanding of the changes happening inside your own skin? How do they bring your experience with God into focus? How do they become models for changes that you still need to make in your own life?

2

BEGINNING
WHERE YOU ARE

THE WORDS ON THE POSTER GRIPPED my imagination: "If you don't know where I've been, you cannot know where I'm coming from." Like everyone else you have roots. You have a past. Your self-image today and the person you become tomorrow is shaped by that past. Your identity makes sense only when you know where you're coming from. And that is especially true of your spiritual development. Who you become *for* Jesus depends upon where you've been *with* him.

Your decision to follow Jesus was a vital one. You will never again be the same. From the moment you first trusted him, God has been working inside your life. This has probably awakened all kinds of emotions within you and you have likely raised some questions about what he is up to. Every new quest involves questions. What exactly has taken place in your life? Where are you coming from spiritually?

The New Testament describes your salvation experience in many different ways. The most common description is that you've been "born again." This phrase comes from Jesus' remark to Nicodemus and literally means to be "born from above" (John 3:3). You have now had a spiritual birth, just as you once had a physical one. This means that life begins anew for you in salvation. You have a new set of options and opportunities for life. The hypothetical question, "If you could live your life over again what would you change?" is no longer theoretical. That question is a real possibility in salvation The Apostle Paul was getting at this when he defined salvation as a process whereby you actually become a new person: "If any man is in Christ, he is a new creature; the old things passed away; behold, new things have come" (2 Cor. 5:17).

Can you identify with these two descriptions? Perhaps deep inside you feel like a new and different person. Maybe you intuitively know that life is beginning all over again for you. Becoming a new person is a real experience. That is what salvation is all about. But how do you become this new person? It doesn't happen automatically. How do you actualize the potential for new life that God has given you? The first step is to understand what has happened thus far in your salvation experience. You need to get a good biblical grasp on where you're coming from with Jesus.

The Bible uses many other pictures to describe what your salvation experience is like. Salvation is being adopted into God's family (Rom. 8:14-17). It is becoming a citizen in some new country (Phil. 3:18-21). It is being found when you are lost (Luke 15). It is running a race (Heb. 12:1-2). It is letting Jesus live in your place (Gal. 2:20). The Bible contains numerous metaphors like these for salvation. Yet, your experience with Jesus is not a metaphor. Metaphors are pictures. Your salvation experience is real. You are actually becoming a new person. The major biblical metaphors for salvation discussed here will serve you as x-rays serve a physician. They picture what is going on inside you. Understanding the metaphors can help you understand your own salvation experience.

Salvation

The noun *salvation* and the verb *to save* are the most common biblical words used to describe the experience of human renewal that we have in God. When the earliest Christians used these words they were not creating new theological terms to spring on their peers. These words had a long history behind them and were widely used in the ancient world. Nor were they particularly religious words. The first Christians merely borrowed them from everyday speech to picture what God had done and was doing in their own lives. Even today I find it helpful to use words like salvation, saved, and savior when I want to talk religion to someone. But what do these words mean? What is the human experience that peeps out from behind them?

Several years ago I made a pastoral call on one of the elderly ladies in my parish. She was one of the substitutes on God's team, for although she had been a church member for years, she had never risked getting involved in what God is up to. She had always watched his action from the sidelines. Now, from a rocking chair on her front porch, she summed up her spiritual pilgrimage in one terse paragraph. "I was saved seventy years ago," she began, "when I was nine years old. I remember it was a revival in late August and very hot. Since that night I haven't been to church a lot, mostly when someone died. And nothing much has changed for me. I still have some of the same fears I had before I was saved. I've still got some of the same bad habits. My life is still very empty. I never did have much to live for, and I still worry a lot about guilt. But, pastor, because of that experience when I was nine I can honestly say, 'Thank God I'm saved!' "

Something inside of me wanted to stand up and shout at that dear lady: "Saved? Saved? Saved from what?" Salvation is not some experience that we have once like getting the measles and then go on living as though nothing had ever happened. Salvation is a vital experience. It is a continuing experience. It is a real process whereby we actually become new persons.

The word translated "salvation" was used in a variety of ways in the ancient world. Yet it always had the basic meaning of "deliverance." It was used in a military sense for political liberation. A general might rescue, or save, a people from their enemies in battle. In such an event he would be called a savior. Salvation was also used in everyday speech to denote rescue from any threatening situation. And it was used as a medical term for deliverance from disease. In this sense, "salvation" meant "health" and the verb "to save" meant "to heal." Such connotations were most appropriate for Jesus, who likened himself to a physician (Mark 2:12).

In the New Testament you will find that the verb *to save* describes deliverance from sin (Matt. 1:21), death (Matt. 8:25), anxiety (Matt. 14:30), danger (Matt 8:35, Acts 27:31), and the infectious influence of an evil environment (Acts 2:40). Of course, deliverance from such as these does not come overnight. There is no instant relief. Salvation, like recovery from any illness, is a process. The New Testament teaches that we "have been saved" (Eph, 2:8), we "are being saved" (1 Cor. 1:18), and that we "will be saved" (Rom. 5:9). The bottom line of all this is quite simple. Salvation is God's process to deliver us from all elements in life which destroy and cripple us. It is a process which leads to health, wholeness, and self-actualization.

Imagine that your life is a shuttle on a straight line. The line moves in two directions. At one end are health and wholeness. Illness, disintegration, and death are at the other end. To move toward the health end is growth. To move in the opposite direction is regression. To remain where you are is fixation. Every decision that you make about your life—how you will respond to situations, how you will make decisions, how you will behave, where you will go, what you will do with your life, how you will handle problems, how you will choose and value—-moves you in one of the two directions on the line. You can choose to live in a manner that diminishes you, that produces all kinds of illnesses— including emotional and spiritual ones. You can choose a lifestyle which disintegrates and fragments your personhood. Or your decisions can move you toward health and wholeness. Your choices can enliven and embellish you as a person. You can become a self-actualizing, authentic individual. The Bible puts it more bluntly; you can move toward life or toward death (Deut. 30:15; Jer. 21:8; Matt. 7:13-14).

Salvation is a way of living that moves you toward health and wholeness. It is a process which, in spite of the flux of daily struggle, increasingly heals you from all elements that dehumanize and destroy you. And no matter where their shuttles happen to be on the straight line continuum, Jesus is able to heal all those who inch closer to God through him (Heb. 7:25).

Justification

What is salvation like? It is like being condemned for some crime and then receiving a free pardon. The Apostle Paul put it this way: "Therefore, since we are justified by faith, we have peace with God through our Lord Jesus Christ" (Rom. 5:1). The word *justification* was originally a legal term. It is used in the New Testament to describe salvation and means "to make just," "to put right," "to acquit," or "to pardon."

Ovid once wrote, "I see the better things, and I agree with them, but I follow the worse." There is a bit of Ovid in each of us, for the Bible describes us in much the same way. We are sinners (Rom. 3:23). We are caught up in an inner conflict between good and evil (Rom. 7:16-21). Inevitably we do what we should not and fail to do what we should (Rom. 7:13-15). And in our most candid moments we know that we stand before God with egg on our moral faces. We are guilty and worthy of death (Rom. 6:23). Yet while we are standing at the bench to receive God's judgment, we receive his pardon instead: "There is therefore now no condemnation for those who are in Christ Jesus" (Rom. 8:1, NAS). God actively involves himself in our lives to start putting things right. That is justification. That is what salvation is like.

Carlyle Marney was once a visiting lecturer at one of the seminaries I attended. A student in one of the classes asked him to wrap up the Christian gospel in one sentence. Marney walked to the board and wrote the following sentence in bold letters: "God is *for* you!" That is the simplest definition I know for justification. God accepts you as you are and puts you into a right relationship with himself.

The experience of justification is graphically illustrated in Jesus' encounter with an adulterous woman (John 8). Some pious Pharisees brought the woman to him; they had caught her living with a man to whom she wasn't married. There was no doubt about her guilt. But there was some question about what to do with her. The Mosaic law called for a punishment of stoning. And the Pharisees were trigger-happy. They wanted to give the woman what the law said she deserved. And they asked Jesus to approve their game plan. For, you see, some of the Pharisees valued the law above everything, even human life. Jesus, however, did not go along with their interest. He ignored them at first, stooping down to trace meaningless figures in the sand with his finger. This act expressed his disgust for the Pharisees' attitude. Yet the Pharisees couldn't take a hint. They kept pressing Jesus about punishing the woman. That is when Jesus unmasked them all with one verbal blow: "Let the one among you who is sinless throw the first stone."

It is interesting that the only ones condemned in this incident were the "good" people. Jesus censured their lack of compassion and caring for the young woman. She was living in open adultery, an act that ran against the very moral fiber in Jewish life. Yet Jesus neither condemned nor condoned her. Instead of judgment, she received forgiveness. Jesus accepted her the way she was and spoke words of pardon: "Neither do I condemn you." Then he created a new possibility for the woman, the possibility of making things right in her life: "Go your way and sin this way no more."

Jesus was for that woman. Although society wanted to throw her away with the trash, she mattered to Jesus. He set her free from the past and became involved in setting things right in her life. She received more than she deserved. And that is what Justification is all about. It is a courtroom word which pictures the judge pardoning and rehabilitating a criminal. In a sense, God does that for you in salvation. He accepts you just as you are. He pardons your past and starts to make things right in your life. He rehabilitates you. He makes you just. God always takes sinners where they are, but he never leaves them where he finds them.

Sanctification

The early church borrowed a family of words from primitive religious cults and used these to picture salvation in terms of behavior. You will find these words on almost every page of the New Testament. Jesus gave his life "to sanctify" the church (Eph. 5:6). You are to be a "consecrated" vessel suited for God's use (2 Tim. 2:20). God wants to establish your life in "holiness" (1 Thess. 3:13). You are to be "holy" as God is holy (I Pet. 1:15). And as a follower of Jesus, you are a "saint" (Col. 1:2; Phil. 1:1; 1 Cor. 1:2). The words *sanctification, saint, holy, holiness,* and *consecration* are all related and mean "dedication" or "separation." The root meaning, however, simply is "to be different."

Two things always stand out when these words are used in the New Testament. Sanctification is God's act. He is the one who separates man from the world and makes him different from what he used to be. And on man's part sanctification always involves behaving in a manner consistent with God's character.

A used-car salesman once told me that his conversion experience created a severe crisis of conscience for him. He was unable to reconcile what he professed on Sunday with his business practices during the rest of the week. "I couldn't sleep nights," he confessed, "until I decided that my religion had nothing to do with my business."

Many of the first-century religious cults danced to that same tune. They separated ethics and religion. Some of the cults demanded ritual purity for brief periods, but few insisted upon a total break with the past. They did not require renunciation of immoral behavior in all areas of life. Seneca, one of the foremost philosophers in that day, spoke out of the moral bankruptcy of such religions when he asked, "Do we know how to live? Do we know how to die?" First-century religions taught men to do neither. They failed to bridge the gap between religion and living. Belief for them had little to do with behavior.

Sanctification is a lifelong process wherein you become holy as God is holy (1 Pet. 1:15). This simply means that you are to be different. Just as God is different from the world, you are to be different from what you used to be and from what the world now is. Your values, morals, and behaviors are to reflect the character of God. And this ethical dimension is to touch every area of your life. It is not just a Sunday affair.

You are now a saint, but that doesn't mean you are sinless. You are to be holy, but that does not mean you are a "holier-than-thou." You are being sanctified, but that does not mean you are a finished product. A saint is one who drops his defenses and leaves himself open to God's influence. He is one who moves in the direction God nudges him. He is working with God to bring all areas of his life under God's control. Some people simply go through life *believing* in Jesus. Sanctification is going through life *behaving* Jesus.

Redemption

There are two metaphors in the Bible which portray salvation as release, liberation, or freedom. These are *ransom* and *redemption*. Jesus said, "The Son of man also came not to be served but to serve, and to give his life as a ransom for many" (Mark 10:45). There are several new Testament passages that speak of our redemption through Jesus' death (Heb. 9:15; Eph. 1:7; and Col. 1:14). We are redeemed from past sins (Rom. 3:24-25), from a rebellious attitude toward God (Titus 2:14), and an empty, meaningless life (I Pet.1:18).

In the ancient world, the words ransom and redemption basically referred to freedom that was effected by the payment of some price. POWs, for instance, were liberated from prison camps by the payment of a ransom (Isa. 45:13). Yet most frequently in the first century, redemption pictured liberation from slavery. A slave would sometimes entrust small amounts of money to a priest of some pagan temple. When enough money was deposited, the priest would purchase the slave in the name of the particular god he served. The slave was then given freedom, but he always considered himself the possession of the god in whose name freedom was purchased. The Apostle Paul used this practice to describe salvation: "You are not your own; You were bought with a price. So glorify God in your body" (1 Cor. 6:19-20).

The early Christians emphasized three truths when they used redemption as a picture for the salvation experience. Man is not free to actualize himself. Salvation is the process whereby man is liberated from all that impedes his growth as a real, fully-alive person. And human liberation is affected by Jesus.

Alexsandr Solzhenitsyn, in *The Gulag Archipelago Three*, tells of one Estonian Georgi Tenno, who was enslaved in a Russian prison camp. Tenno repeatedly tried to escape, only to be caught and returned to his cell. Other prisoners continued to ask him what he expected to find on the outside. Tenno's reply was always the same, "Freedom, of course! A whole day in the taiga without chains—that's what I call freedom!"[2]

What do you call freedom? In what ways have you been set free by your experience with Jesus? Where in your life do you still need liberation? The gospel message is that Jesus sets you free for freedom (Gal. 6:1).

I once followed a student across campus. He wore a T-shirt with the statement "Jesus Means Freedom." He most certainly does! And his freedom involves more than one day in the taiga without chains.

Eternal Life

The words *eternal life* and *life* are both used in the New Testament to describe what salvation is. Contrary to popular opinion, eternal life does not refer primarily to life that goes on and on without end. It is true that eternal life never ceases, but the emphasis is on the *quality* of the life lived now instead of the *quantity* of life gained after death. As such, eternal life means two things for you in your search for meaning.

Eternal life means living in fellowship with God in the midst of this life. Jesus defined eternal life as simply "knowing" God (John 17:3). The act of knowing him is maintaining a personal relationship with him. You know God in much the same way that you come to know another person--by sharing life together and by revealing your inmost selves to one another. In this way you come to *know* God, and not just know about him. Personal relationships always give depth and meaning to life, and this is especially true with reference to God. Eternal life is sharing life with God, living in fellowship with him here and now.

Eternal life also means sharing the life *of* God. The New Testament teaches that God is not confined by temporal limitations (2 Pet. 3:8). God dwells in eternity, and because of this he sometimes is called the Eternal. Eternal life is nothing less than the life of God himself. The call given for man to share eternal life is a call to participate in God's life in Christ (John 3:13-21). His life is purposeful and meaningful. Man shares in purpose and meaning when he shares life *with* God and when he shares the life *of* God.

When a person aligns himself with a world opposed to God, he participates in death, because the world is passing away (Eph. 2:1-5; 1 John 2:16-17). When one aligns himself with God, he participates in life and meaning. This is life *from* God (Eph. 2:5), *for* God (Eph. 2:10), but most of all, it is life *with* God.

My wife was sitting in the office of an orthodontist one day and overheard two women talking about the advantages of swimming. One lady remarked, "Everyone ought to know how to swim. What if you were caught in a flood? You'd have to be able to swim to survive your life!"

The woman's slip of the tongue uncovered a truth far deeper than she realized. Life tumbles in on top of us at times. Sometimes the pain of living is almost unbearable. Daily routine becomes drudgery. Dorothy Sayers once remarked that the real problem of life is that it is so everlastingly daily. At times the question literally stares you in the face: "How can you survive your life?"

Victor Frankl was a Viennese psychiatrist who survived years of agony in a Nazi concentration camp during World War II. He suffered every way a person can suffer short of death. Yet through his experiences he gained a new slant on life that has influenced many people. Wholeness and health do not come to you in the absence of pain and suffering. If that were so you would never experience wholeness, for no one lives without suffering. Wholeness and health come from meaning and purpose in your life. If you have a *why* to live, you can endure almost any *what*. Have you ever heard of a person's dying for no other reason than that he or she lost the will to live?

The Bible also affirms that you can become a whole person only when you have a *why* for living. Meaningfulness in life is necessary for health. The Bible calls this meaningful existence eternal life.

Can you notice a qualitative difference in your life

since you started following Jesus? He gives you something to live for. He is someone to live for. He can indeed enable you to survive your life.

Reconciliation

Reconciliation, which literally means "a restoration to fellowship," is one of the words Paul used to describe what salvation is all about. According to the Bible, the human predicament is one of fragmentation and estrangement. Man is divided deep *within* himself *from* himself. He struggles to find and maintain his own integrity, to know who he is and why he is. And on the *outside,* man is separated from others, uninvolved in the scheme of things, isolated and alone. He must use words like *hostility, war, manipulation, apathy, greed,* and *alienation* to describe human relationships. Yet, from the depths of his being, man recognizes his plight and struggles for unity.

Of course, *man* is just a synonym for *you.* Man's predicament is your predicament. Have you not experienced the fragmentation of human existence? Do you know what it means to be separated from God, from your fellows, and from yourself? And do you experience the frustration of not being able to "put it all together"?

Reconciliation is the nemesis of fragmentation. It is God's way of "putting it all together," of bringing man into harmony with himself and with the rest of creation. In 2 Corinthians 5:15-6:10, reconciliation depicts the total process of salvation; it is synonymous with the "new creation" (2 Cor. 5:17). Both concepts—reconciliation and new creation—designate a new way of existing in relation to God and others.

Paul, in this text, made five observations about reconciliation: (1) Reconciliation is always God's act (2 Cor. 5:18). Just as God brought *all* creation into being, only he can bring about the new creation. (2) Man is the object of reconciliation (2 Cor. 5:18-19). Man is the one who needs to be reconciled. Man is the one who is out of harmony with God and his fellows. (3) God reconciles men through Christ (2 Cor. 5:18, 21). When Jesus' teachings are followed, and when the significance of his death is realized, wholeness replaces fragmentation. (4) Reconciliation is God's act of accepting men in spite of their sins (2 Cor. 5:19). God does not hold grudges against you because of your past misdeeds. Rather, he prefers to hold you in close relationship with himself. (5) The result of being reconciled is becoming involved in the reconciling process (2 Cor. 5:20–6:10).

Where Are You Coming From?

Every journey begins for you where you are. This especially is true regarding your spiritual pilgrimage. Where are you corning from spiritually? What have you really experienced in Jesus?

Frank Stagg captured the essence of your experience, as well as the nature of the words used to describe salvation, when he wrote that redemption can be viewed from different angles.[3] For one who has lost his way, salvation is *direction.* It is *reconciliation* for those who are alienated. It is forgiveness for those who are guilty. It is *liberation* for those bound by such things as prejudice, hate, lust, greed, guilt, or fear. It is *strength* for those who are not up to what life demands. It is *meaning* for those who have no reason to live. It is *sanctification* for those who place themselves at God's disposal. It is *resurrection* for those who have come alive for the first time. It is *justification* for those whom God is rehabilitating. Salvation is becoming a real person—fully alive in the presence of God, in the presence of others, and in your own presence.

3

SALVATION IS
GOD'S GIFT TO YOU

EVERY DAY I BECOME MORE CONVINCED that life comes
gift wrapped. You did not ask for life. Your parents gave it
to you. And that was only the beginning! Everything worth
having in this world, everything that gives zip to existence,
is free. I am referring to such things as love, acceptance,
caring, affection, friendship, beauty, and intimacy. To be a
healthy person you need these as much as you need oxygen
and vitamins. Yet none of these can be bought. If you
possess them at all it is because someone freely gives them
to you. Paul Tournier really put his finger on our pulse
when he said that "we all hunger for gifts as we hunger for
universal and limitless love, for gifts are signs of that
compelling and deep-seated desire to love and be loved." [4]

The Bible describes your experience of salvation with words like *justification, reconciliation, sanctification,* and *redemption.* But when it speaks of salvation from God's position, it uses words like *mercy, grace,* and *gift.* You are born anew in Jesus "according to (God's abundant mercy) (1 Pet. 1:3 KJV). The word translated "according to" is almost an equivalent to our mathematical phrase "in proportion to." The salvation you have experienced is not in proportion to your own good works or achievement. It is not in proportion to what you can merit on your own. Your experience is far greater than anything you can muster up yourself. Salvation is in proportion to God's mercy. And mercy, of course, has no price tag. It cannot be bought. It can only be given.

Salvation is also a possibility for all men because of God's grace. The New Testament declares that we experience grace in Jesus (1 Cor. 1:4). This is because Jesus is the embodiment of grace: "The law was given through Moses; grace and truth came through Jesus Christ. No one has ever seen God; the only Son, who is in the bosom of the Father, he has made him known" (John 1:17-18). The phrase "made him known" literally means "to translate the meaning of one language into another." Jesus translated God into terms we can all understand. He put God in the vernacular. Consequently, if you want to know what God is like, look at Jesus. And when you look at him you will see grace in action. Jesus cared for people. He accepted sinners. He forgave the guilty. He healed the sick. He consoled those who hurt. He comforted the lonely. Jesus *did* that because God *does* that. In Jesus, God offers himself *to* us and *for* us. That is grace. And that kind of giving cannot be purchased. It can only be received.

The Bible never minces words about the gospel. God effects salvation. People experience salvation. God is the one who saves. You are the one who is saved. Salvation is always God's activity. Man is always on the receiving end. God gives salvation. It is his gift to you. And that is precisely what makes the good news *good*.

Paul Tournier, in *The Meaning of Gifts*, reminds us that we humans have an insatiable thirst for both giving and receiving gifts. The gifts themselves are mostly unimportant. What is important is that they symbolize our need for love and affirmation. And although our use of gifts is sometimes motivated by pride, self-interest, or an attempt to manipulate others, the quest for gifts is our quest for love. At the deepest level, our use of gifts is a seeking after God. For he is the one who made all things, and he is the only one who can truly give without asking anything in return except gratitude.

This certainly echoes a familiar refrain in the Bible. God offers himself to you in Jesus. His gift of salvation demonstrates that he is vitally interested in you. It is evidence that he loves you with no reservations. Salvation is just another word for God accepting you unconditionally: "For by grace you have been saved through faith; and this is not your own doing, it is the gift of God" (Eph. 2:8). The word "it" in the last statement refers to the entire process of salvation. From beginning to end, salvation is God's gift to you.

Grace Is Something God Does

The words *mercy, grace,* and *gift* mean essentially the same thing. They underline in bold strokes that salvation is God's doing. You cannot earn the new life in Jesus any more than you work every day to earn the privilege of living the next. Salvation is by grace. But what does that mean?

One of the most prominent features of our faith is that all the great nouns we celebrate—*justice, mercy, truth, love, faith, grace, good*—are also verbs. They are not abstract ideas or ways of feeling. They are ways of behaving. According to the gospels, you as a Christian are to do justice (Matt. 23:23). You are to do mercy (Luke 10:37). You are to do faith (Matt. 23:23). You are to do the truth (John 3:21). And you are to do the good (Luke 5:35). The same is true for grace. For, like all the others, grace is something you do.

Jesus once said, "If you love those who love you, what credit is that to you? For even sinners love those who love them. And if you do good to those who do good to you, what credit is that to you? For even sinners do the same. And if you lend to those from whom you hope to receive, what credit is that to you?" (Luke 6:32-34). The question translated "what credit is that to you?" literally means "what grace is in you?" Grace, in this quotation, is a way of behaving. It means doing what is best for someone else whether they deserve it or not. It is acting in the best interests of the other fellow rather than your own.

As you read the gospels, you will notice that Jesus seldom used the word *grace*. Yet the Bible states that grace became a reality through him (John 1:16-17). Jesus did not talk grace; he did grace. It was grace in action when he ate with tax collectors and sinners. It was grace when he healed the sick. It was grace when he forgave sins. Jesus never catered just to good and deserving people. He never asked a person for his moral credentials before loving him. Whereas the Pharisees associated with sinners only after they reformed, Jesus accepted people before they improved themselves. He accepted all persons because his grace was for each person.

Jesus created grace by behaving grace toward people. And the good news is that God acts the same way. You and

I are sinners. We disobey God not because we have to, but because we want to, yet God does not live by the "eye for an eye" principle. He does not treat us the way we treat him. He turns the other cheek; he goes the second mile with us; he forgives us over and over again, even when we promise him firmly that we will reform. Rather than condemn us to death as sinners, he died for us. Salvation is God's way of acting in our best interests even though we don't deserve it. Grace is what he does for us through Jesus (1 Cor. 1:4).

Grace Is God Accepting You

Dietrich Bonhoeffer called Jesus a "man for others." That is a most accurate description. He *was* a man for others. Every page of the gospels footnotes this fact. He always acted in the best interests of the persons he met. And the story is still the same. Jesus is *for* people; he is *for* you.

Alice was twenty-three years old and severely disturbed when she walked into my office for her first counseling session. She was the product of a very unhealthy home environment. Her father, the only person whoever expressed any affection for her, had died when she was nine. She was still angry at him for deserting her. Alice's mother was an uncaring person. She seldom manifested interest in any of her children. She was a nominal Christian, but was careful never to let her "faith" influence how she behaved. No matter how hard she tried, Alice was never able to gain her mother's love, care, or respect. She couldn't even get her mother's attention, although she tried with some rather bizarre behaviors. At twenty-three she was an insecure, unloved, unwanted and lonely emotional cripple. She sat on the edge of her chair and literally sobbed out her hurt. Her entire life had become a hopeless crusade to find love and affection. Her repertory of love-deficiency behaviors was most impressive—promiscuity, drug abuse, shoplifting, forgery, drunkenness, prostitution, attempted suicide. "I am rotten," she cried over and over. "I am trash. No one wants me. No one loves me. No one accepts me."

Does God love people like Alice? Does he want them? Or does God care only for the goody-types? Perhaps there is a feeling inside yourself that vibrates to Alice's words. Our world is overpopulated with lonely, hurting, and guilt-ridden people who feel unwanted, unloved, and unworthy. Sister Margaret Theresa of Bangladesh once remarked that to be unloved, unwanted, and uncared for is the greatest sickness in the world today. If there is a small Alice crying out deep within you, behind all the emotional barriers you've built to disguise yourself, then hear the gospel again: God accepts you where you are and just as you are. Jesus died for sinners. Grace is another way of saying that God accepts you with no strings attached.

Grace Is God Valuing You

In Flannery O'Conner's novel *Wise Blood*, Haze, a self-ordained minister in his own church, remarked to a friend as he violently pushed him from an automobile, "My church is the church without Christ. I've seen all of you I want to." That statement sums up life for a lot of people. But it also pinpoints a sore spot in our society. Sometimes people don't matter to us. We have developed a funny notion that a person is not worth much unless he has scored some points in the system, or has a certain talent, or does something really worthwhile. We value people conditionally. They are important *because*; they are worthwhile *because*. Not only are we conditioned to think this way, we silently get the message across to others that live with us. I painfully discovered this a short time ago with my son. We were driving into town, and right out of the blue I hit him with a "warm fuzzy." That's psychology talk for a stroke, an unsolicited affirmation. I simply told him what I was feeling for him at that moment. "Art, I really like you," I said. His immediate response was, "Why?" It was then that I realized that unconsciously I had programmed him to believe that he was OK only when he behaved OK. It was difficult for him to understand that I could like him just for himself!

I have a need to be valued and accepted for no reason at all other than I'm me. And I think you have the same need.

Everybody needs to be *somebody*. We come that way from the factory. We come alive when we are valued unconditionally. Without that kind of affirmation each of us is just a person-that-might-have-been. Can you imagine how it feels when your spouse walks in and says, "I don't want you any more"? Do you know what happens inside the child who runs to a parent bubbling over with excitement only to be shoved aside with a "don't bother me now"? Do you know what it is like when people ignore you in a conversation or belittle your ideas and suggestions? Have you ever looked at someone you love and wished to God that he (or she) would give some indication that he cares? Can you remember what it was like on the playground when the kids chose up sides for a game and you were chosen last? Everyone needs to matter to someone. Everyone needs to feel that they count, that they are of value. The good news about salvation is that you matter to Jesus. Grace is God valuing you as a person.

Jesus valued people above everything else. It didn't matter about their race, or their economic status, or their moral pedigree. All people mattered to him. He taught that people are more important than animals (Matt. 6:26). He believed that any person mattered more than the entire material world (Matt. 16:26). He told all who would listen that God valued people more than sacrifices (Man. 5:23-24), Sabbath-day rituals (Mark 2:23-27), or religious traditions (John 3:3-11).

I think that Jesus' table manners betrayed his interest in people more than anything else he did. He would eat with anyone. And in his day that was very significant. Table fellowship in the first century was a closely guarded ritual. The table represented friendship, intimacy, brotherhood, and acceptance. In Jesus' day, one ate only with those he accepted. One never ate with his enemies or those considered to be in a lower caste. It just wasn't kosher to violate the soundness of the table tradition. That is why the meal was especially significant for Jesus. He forbade no one to sit at his table. He would break bread with anyone. And it was for this reason he was branded as one who ate with tax collectors and sinners (Mark 2:16).

The Pharisees refused to eat with people they considered trash. Jesus' table manners for them was a *dis*grace. But for Jesus his manners were simply grace. The act of eating with sinners was his way of accepting them. He made no prior demands upon them. He required nothing from them. His willingness to sit at the table with them was grace in action. He did not condone how the sinners lived. But he did value them as persons.

Perhaps table manners are one way we can measure the genuineness and depth of our faith. Whom are you willing to eat with? Whom do you exclude from your table? And on what basis do you exclude them? Jesus excluded no one. He excludes no one today. He invites you as well as Alice to sit with him. That's because he values people. That is what grace means.

Grace Is God Saving You

Abraham Heschel, a prominent Jewish theologian, has remarked that there are more songs in the human heart than the tongue can utter. I know what he means! More songs are deep within than one can express, and Christians well may add that Jesus sets them all to music. At least, this was so for the author of Ephesians. He began his letter with one of those songs, a liturgical hymn of praise to God for his gracious activity on behalf of man (Eph. 1:3-14).

The hymn itself celebrates the work of the Father, the Son, and the Holy Spirit in providing redemption, a work whereby wholeness is restored to human existence. The hymn contains three stanzas, and each stanza is followed by the same basic chorus: "To the praise of his glory" (Eph. 1:6, 12, 14).

The Father is celebrated in the first stanza of the hymn as one who elects men to appear before him and who foreordains them to be his sons (Eph. 1:4-6). Both of these activities were "before the foundation of the world" (Eph. 1:4), prior to all human history and natural processes. Clearly, redemption is not God's afterthought nor man's invention. Redemption proceeds solely from the will of the Father (Eph. 1:3-5).

The Father's purpose in election and foreordination (concepts that are intended to emphasize God's grace and initiative in salvation) is to adopt men as his sons (Eph. 1:5). Sonship certainly does not imply divinity on man's part, but it is expressive of the dynamic way Hebrews thought. The word refers to a way of living in harmony with God. Sonship, first of all means obedience to God. In biblical thought the son always was expected to obey his father (Eph. 6:1; Col. 3:20). This is the idea in Jesus' statement that only children can enter God's kingdom (Mark 10:15). One exists as God's son when he obeys God as Father. Also, the phrase "son of" was a Hebrew colloquial expression denoting character. A man was called the "son of" whatever characterized his life. James and John were called "sons of thunder" because they had stormy dispositions (Mark 3:17). Jesus called the Pharisees sons of the devil, because they sometimes acted like the devil (John 8:38, 44). Thus, to be a son of God means to act in a way consistent with his character, to share his concerns in daily behavior (Luke 6:32-36). The words *holy, blameless,* and *loving* partially describe that which is in character with him (Eph. 1:4). The Father's desire that men appear "before" him (Eph. 1:4) does not mean to stand in his presence as sons at the end of history. It means to live in his presence now. Life is to be celebrated now as an occasion of joy and as an opportunity to engage the problems of this age creatively.

The second stanza of the hymn praises the Son for redeeming men and forgiving their trespasses (Eph. 1:7-12). Redemption is a concept that derives, in part, from the practice of sacral manumission. Manumission was an ancient custom whereby slaves were emancipated from bondage by the payment of a certain price to the owners. The word also referred to the liberation of war prisoners by a ransom paid to their captors. The focal point of both acts of "redemption" was the emancipation that was effected. This is the emphasis of all New Testament passages that use redemption as a model for salvation. Jesus sets men free, a liberation movement for everyone.

The text is explicit about forgiveness. Jesus forgives men their trespasses (Eph. 1:7). Forgiveness literally means "to send away" or "dismiss." The verb translated "forgive" is used in a variety of ways in the New Testament, even to mean divorce (1 Cor, 7:11-12). This latter usage stresses thorough separation. Forgiveness, when used in connection with sin, means the actual loosing of an individual from his sins. It is the removal of all barriers hindering a proper relationship with God. More than a mere exchange of words between God and man, or "cheap grace" as Dietrich Bonhoeffer called it, forgiveness is a creative act whereby man is set free *from* sin and set free *for* God. This, too, is in proportion to Gods grace and not human effort (Eph. 1:7).

But from what are men liberated? The text does not say, yet this silence accentuates an important truth. The New Testament never limits that from which man is liberated. In Ephesians alone, Paul spoke of liberation from ignorance (1:18), disobedience (2:1-3), alienation (2:11-12), and hopelessness (2:11-12). Man is liberated from all things that contribute to a futile and purposeless existence (compare Eph. 4:17-24 and I Pet 1:18). Jesus effected this liberation through his death (Eph. 1:7).

The Holy Spirit is celebrated in the final stanza for sealing believers (Eph. 1:13) and assuring their ultimate redemption (Eph. 1:14). "Sealing," the practice of placing an identifying mark upon some article, was an Oriental custom designating ownership or authenticity. Here it means that one's redemption is authenticated when the Holy Spirit is present in his life. Simultaneously, the Holy Spirit becomes the guarantee of one's inheritance or redemption (Eph. 1:14). *Guarantee* translates a word used to refer to an initial payment in a business transaction that certifies the full contract will be carried out. The presence of the Holy Spirit in a person's life is God's promise (guarantee) that redemption in all of its fulness will be completed in the future.

This hymn of praise celebrates the entire message of the Bible— that God alone is responsible for your salvation. The Father initiates salvation, the Son accomplishes salvation, and the Holy Spirit consummates salvation. From beginning to end, salvation is totally God's doing. He *provides* redemption; man *participates* in redemption. All, therefore, is to the praise of his glory. Grace is God's act of saving you.

Grace Is God's Gift

A few years ago I came down with a bad case of the Jonah complex. I started running out on God. Not the church, mind you! I continued to play my professional roles as minister and teacher. I just wanted to get away from God. So I wore the masks and played the game. It was easy at first, but inside I was slowly drying up. I was a phony and I knew it! The game went on for months and then everything began falling apart. All the air finally leaked out of my spiritual balloon. The luster faded from my personal relationships. My family took a back seat. God became my enemy. I was dying on the vine and I wanted out. Out of my vocation. Out of my friendships. Out of the church. And as far away from God as I could get.

The only way I knew to get out was to run. So that is precisely what I did. I enrolled in a secular university and began preparing for a new vocation. I felt I didn't need God anymore and I didn't want the church. I made a solemn oath inside my head that as soon as I retooled vocationally I would bail out of the ministry. But then the unexpected happened. God took me by surprise. For, like Jonah, the farther I ran away from God the closer I got to him. One day, hurrying to a class along with twenty-five thousand other bodies, I ran into Jesus. I don't mean literally. But he was there. It was real. And he spoke to me. He whispered, "Bill, I know you don't love me anymore. I know you don't want me anymore. I just wanted you to know that I still love you." That was the moment I learned what grace feels like. That was the day I began to recover. For that day I met Jesus again and I knew deep down inside that salvation is God's gift of grace.

4

SALVATION IS GOD'S DEMAND UPON YOU

I ONCE HEARD THE STORY OF A MAN who rededicated his life to the Lord during a revival meeting. He said to the congregation, "You all know that I've committed every sin in the book. I've gambled, beat my wife and kids, and spent time in jail for drunkenness and fighting. I've done it all. But thank God that through all my sinful living I never once lost my religion!"

I don't know what kind of Christianity that man had, but it certainly wasn't genuine. Real faith embraces how you behave as well as what you believe.

Eberhard Arnold was an influential Christian in Germany at the turn of the 20th century. On one occasion he wrote to his future bride, "I am so *very* glad that you too love so much to see *Jesus* always in the center. That alone is healthy Christianity. Not teaching, but *Jesus*; not feelings, but *Jesus*; not effort, but *Jesus*! Always, nothing but His will, His peace, and His power!"

The Bible is very clear in affirming that salvation is ours by God's grace. It is his gift. Yet sometimes those of us in the church play the grace record so often we seldom hear what is on the flip side—real salvation demands radical obedience to Jesus. Here is the paradox of faith that you must reconcile in your own life. You are not saved by your obedience to God. Yet you are truly saved only when you live in obedience to God. Dietrich Bonhoeffer put it bluntly: "Only he who believes is obedient, and only he who is obedient believes."

You should not interpret this to mean you will never sin or that you are not a real Christian if you do sin. All saints are sinners. This does mean, however, that authentic faith involves radical obedience to God as he is revealed in Jesus Christ.

Jesus and Obedience

The simplest way I know to define salvation is that it is living in obedience to Jesus. This doesn't mean you are saved by what you do. It is merely an acknowledgment that there is no real salvation apart from obedience to him. The author of Hebrews was affirming this very point when he said of Jesus, "he became the source of eternal salvation to all who obey him" (Heb. 5:9). This is why James wrote that real faith always involves obedience (James 2:17). Salvation is both God's gift to you and his demand upon you. He demands obedience. His grace is free, but it is not cheap. It cost the life of his only son (1 Pet. 1:18-21), and it also requires your life (Matt. 16:24-25).

Jesus always focused upon God's demand for obedience when he spoke to people about salvation. You will find in the gospels that he invariably summoned men to salvation with the same words: "Follow me!" He issued this call to four fishermen (Matt. 4:19-22), a tax collector (Matt. 9:9), three anonymous individuals (Luke 9:57-60), and two young lawyers (Matt. 19:16-22; Luke 10:25-37). The individuals were different, but the call was always the same. First, Jesus' call was an imperative. "Follow me" is a command. And there are only two possible responses you can give to a command. You can either obey or disobey. The same was true for you when Jesus called you to salvation. You began to experience his redeeming grace when you first obeyed his call. The salvation journey always begins with obedience to Jesus' call.

Jesus' call to discipleship also involved a break with the past for all who followed him. The new life he offers demands new values and behavior. You cannot completely follow Jesus while you cling desperately to old loyalties. You cannot fully become a new person as long as you live like your old self. This is why Jesus said, "No one who puts his hand to the plow and looks back is fit for the kingdom of God" (Luke 9:62).

Jesus' call to salvation involved a radical commitment to himself. His command is always, "Follow *me!*" Jesus is the center of healthy Christianity. Salvation is not believing a set of doctrines. It is not committing yourself to an ethical system. Salvation is a relationship to a person. In the first century, real discipleship meant following Jesus. And it still does.

Finally, Jesus' call, "Follow me, meant to live a certain way. The verb translated "follow" means to live by his teachings, to be involved in his manner of living. A true disciple places himself under Jesus' discipline. This can be illustrated very simply. You "follow" a physician's orders when you do what he prescribes. You "follow" a friend's suggestion when you actually do what he says. You "follow" a set of instructions when you carry cut the step-by-step directions they provide. And you follow Jesus the same way. To follow Jesus is to live by his teachings and model his behavior. You follow Jesus when you practice what he preached. Obedience to Jesus' call is the only entrance to the life road.

Jesus taught over and over again that real disciples cannot continually believe one way and behave another. Salvation always involves obedience. Only those who do God's will enjoy the blessing of salvation (Matt. 7:21). The real Christian is one who builds his life upon obedience to Jesus' teachings (Matt. 7:24). Jesus' real family is composed of those who join him in obeying God (Mark 3:31-35). An authentic believer is known by his behavior (Matt. 7:20). One makes a genuine disciple when he teaches that disciple to obey what Jesus taught (Matt. 28:20). Jesus put God's demand for obedience in capital letters when he defined salvation as a practice instead of a profession: "Not every one who says to me, 'Lord, Lord' shall enter the kingdom of heaven, but he who does the will of my Father who is in heaven" (Matt. 7:21). Those of us in the church could learn something from doctors and lawyers. Your family doctor does not profess medicine; he practices it. And he calls his business a practice. Lawyers do not profess the law; they practice it. And they also call their business a practice. If we talk about what it means to be a real follower of Jesus, the question is not, "Are you a professing Christian?" but, "Are you a practicing Christian?" Salvation is a practice; it involves *doing* God's will. It is confessing with your life as well as your mouth that "Jesus Christ is Lord!"

Believing and Behaving

James Moffatt, an influential Christian scholar of another generation, once said that there are two groups of people in every congregation--a large group of persons who believe they believe, and a smaller group who really believe. His point is very important. All belief is not alike. Saving belief is different from intellectual belief.

Belief is a vital factor in your relationship with God. There is no salvation without it: "For God so loved the world that he gave his only Son, that whoever believes in him should not perish but have eternal life" (John 3:15). Yet the word "believe" that appears in your Bible does not mean intellectual belief when it refers to salvation. Faith and belief are synonymous in English, but there is more to that than meets the eye.

Four observations are necessary for a proper understanding of the New Testament word "faith." First, the New Testament mentions various kinds of faith. Not all faith is saving faith, faith through which grace is effective (Luke 8:11-15).Whenever one speaks of faith in relationship to salvation, he should be aware that he is speaking of a particular kind of faith.

A second observation is that faith is volitional; it relates to man's will, not only to his mind, This means that faith, like grace, is active, a way of relating oneself to God.

In a real sense, one does not have faith; one does faith (Matt, 23:23). The Greek language has a verb for faith which the English language does not have. As a result, the verb is translated in most English versions of the New Testament by the English verb "believe" (Mark 1:15; John 3:16). In the original New Testament sense, however, faith is not primarily an intellectual process. It is the total response of the whole person to God.

As far as definitions are concerned, faith basically means "to commit" or "to trust" This is the third important observation about saving faith. One has faith in God, not when he believes certain truths about God, but when he commits his entire life to God. The verb translated "faith" is used most often this way in the New Testament. Jesus, for instance, once refused to entrust himself to those desiring a political messiah (John 2:24). Paul, on one occasion, spoke of knowing the one to whom he had committed his life (2 Tim. 1:12). Saving faith always involves the commitment of life to God.

A fourth observation about saving faith is that it also means obedience. The verb itself is a synonym for obedience (Matt. 21:32). The common New Testament injunction to "believe in" Jesus (John 1:12; 3:15-21; Acts 16:31; Rom. 10:9-10) was based upon a common religious statement during the first century A.D. which always meant "to obey." "Belief in" Jesus means nothing less than obedience to Jesus. This relationship between faith and obedience is always stressed in the New Testament. Paul wrote of the obedience that is faith (Rom. 1:5). James seemed to equate faith and works (James 2:14-25) and made the remarkable statement that one is justified by works (James 2:24). James clearly meant that saving faith always involves obedience.

In the light of these four observations, what is saving faith? True faith is commitment to the point of obedience. A person may commit himself to various points as far as God is concerned. Commitment may be only to the point of believing things about God, attending church, or even memorizing a Bible verse each day. All of these may be types of faith, but they are not saving faith. True faith is the radical submission of oneself to God in openness and trust, a submission in which all other loyalties are subordinated and ultimate allegiance is given only to God. When a person commits himself to this extent, God's grace becomes effective; salvation becomes a reality.

Reasons for Obeying Jesus

There is a question lurking behind all of this obedience talk that ought to be brought out into the open. Why should you obey Jesus? You do not obey in order to gain salvation. It is God's gift. You do not obey out of some legalistic sense to keep divine laws. God has more important things to do than give you a bundle of arbitrary laws and expect you to obey them just because he says so. He is a better parent than that! Why then should you obey Jesus?

You should obey Jesus because that is the nature of salvation. Salvation is not a theological game that simply requires your giving mental assent to all the right things. You can believe all the Bible and still be far from God. Even the devils believe all that is true, but they are still lost (James 2:19). Salvation is more than just believing and having a walk, either mentally or literally, down the sawdust trail. It is a lifelong process. Salvation is a way of living under God's lordship. This is why Jesus and all the New Testament writers stressed that real faith involves obedience to God. You should obey Jesus because that is what salvation is all about. There is no salvation apart from obedience. That is why Bonhoeffer said that only those who believe can obey.

You should obey Jesus because that is the only way you will understand his teachings. I remember counseling a young woman who was going through a divorce, As part of the counseling process, I explored with her what she could expect as a single parent and a divorcee. Some weeks later she confessed to me, "When we talked about what I would experience as a divorcee, I heard what you said with my mind. Now that I live with it every day, I really understand what you were talking about."

Sometimes what people tell us comes alive only when we experience what they say. And this is particularly true in our spiritual pilgrimage. You can learn very much about Jesus' teachings by reading commentaries and religious literature. You can increase your understanding of his sayings by listening to sermons and lectures. But you really know what he was talking about when you transpose his talk into your walk. His words come alive with meaning when you practice them in your daily life.

I used to teach a course on Jesus' teachings in the college where I am employed. Students who wrote term papers in this course were required to do their paper on only one of Jesus' teachings. Their paper involved three phases. *First*, they researched the teaching in the theological literature available in the library. This gave them an intellectual understanding of the text. *Second*, they followed a set of guidelines in practicing the teaching in their own life-setting for one month. During this period they kept a diary of their experiences and feelings. *Third*, they integrated the results of their academic research and practical experience, and wrote their paper using both to interpret Jesus teaching.

Jesus always talked about life. His teachings instruct

us in how to live. They are not intended as texts to memorize or as launching pads for sermons. They are intended to guide our behavior in real life situations. For this reason, I am convinced that you really understand what he taught only when you practice it in your life. This is why Bonhoeffer said that those who obey can believe.

You should obey Jesus because there is healing in his words. The disciples once admitted to Jesus that they followed him because he alone had "the words of life"' (John 6:68). That phrase literally means "words that give life." That is exactly what they do, but not automatically. They produce life when you obey then.

Imagine that you are sick and go to the doctor. Several things will happen during your visit. The doctor will gather verbal information from you. He will ask how you feel, or where you hurt, and you will respond with a list of symptoms. Then he will collect data from his own examination. He will check your blood pressure and your pulse, take your temperature, and the like. On the basis of all the information he collects, the doctor will diagnose what's wrong with you. Then he will prescribe some way for you to recover health. Perhaps he will give you a prescription and say something like, "Get plenty of rest, drink lots of fluids, and take one of these pills after every meal."

You can believe that you are sick and that you have whatever the doctor said you have. You can believe that the medicine and rest he recommends will help you feel better. Yet his words and your belief do not alone produce health. You begin to recover when you do what the doctor says. You get well when you follow his prescription!

It works the same way with Jesus. For not all of our diseases are physical ones. At different times and in various degrees, we suffer emotional, mental, and spiritual illnesses as well. And because our bodies, minds, and spirits are inseparably bound, what affects us in one area usually affects us all over. The Bible frequently warns us about the damages of greed, lust, hostility, bitterness, grudge-bearing, selfishness, and the like. All of these are emotional and volitional germs that contribute to illness. They poison our systems just as severely as any chemical toxin. Sometimes you and I get sick because we think sick and act sick. But how do you go about treating these kinds of diseases? What medicines do you use?

Jesus likened himself to a physician. The entire purpose of his ministry was to save (heal) persons, to make them whole. His teachings are like a doctor's prescription. His words produce life and health when you practice them in particular instances in your own life. How do you cure hostility and hatred? Jesus offers an antidote. It is agape love. You can find healing from particular instances of hatred if you behave loving acts instead of hostile ones. How do you cure particular attacks of greed or selfishness? You do so by doing what Jesus taught about giving and going the second mile. What is the remedy for bitterness and grudge-bearing? Relief is spelled "f-o-r-g-i-v-e-n-e-s-s-." Healing in particular instances comes when you practice what Jesus said about forgiving seventy times seven. And what is true with these particular spiritual illnesses is true of all others.

I keep using the word "particular" for an obvious reason. Practicing love toward one person does not cure us from hostility towards every person. Nor does being healed from bitterness in one situation make us immune to bitterness in all other situations for the rest of our lives. We are always subject to infection again. Seldom does one prescription last a lifetime. Jesus' teachings, however, are potent whenever we need them. Whenever you have an attack of some disease-producing emotion or behavior, there is some antidote in Jesus' teachings which, if practiced as prescribed, will produce health.

There is also one other point worth noting. Jesus' words do not always produce instantaneous healing. One act of love may not vanquish your hostility any more than one aspirin will always alleviate your headache. Jesus' teachings produce health when you follow them continuously.

Perhaps these few examples will give you some idea of what I'm getting at. Jesus' teachings, as well as all God's other commandments, are practical in nature. There is nothing esoteric, theological, or arbitrary about them. They all apply to life where you live it. Jesus' teachings touch on all those areas you struggle with from day to day. He deals with relationships that have gone sour. He talks about fantasies and feelings that bump inside your head causing inner guilt, and self-doubt. He tells you how you can live life instead of letting life live you. He touches upon grief, hurt, and loneliness and offers some handles so you can cope with them. Jesus has some life-giving words. They will do you a world of good when you behave them as well as believe them. You should obey Jesus because there is healing in his words. And, after all, health is what the word salvation literally means.

Living under Jesus' Control

Years ago, our family packed the bare necessities into our station wagon and set out on a private odyssey to explore the West. I still remember the day we stopped to have lunch at a roadside park in Montana. The park was beautifully nestled alongside a river. I hurried through my sandwich and began to meander upstream looking at rocks and trying to imagine what it was like in the "old" days. Several hundred yards upstream I saw it. Someone had the audacity to put some religious graffiti in an out-of-the-way place on a large dull gray rock. The white letters literally blared out the message:

Let Jesus control your life.

You will *never* be sorry.

Upon returning to the car, I noticed a historical marker. Late in the 1800s gold had been discovered a quarter mile downstream in that very river. That discovery started a gold rush in Montana.

As we drove down the highway, I couldn't get the two messages out of my mind. They rummaged through my head like pieces of a puzzle that do not seem to fit. That's when the thought caught my imagination and wouldn't let go. The truth in the graffiti was worth more than all the gold ever panned out of that mountain stream. Live under Jesus' control. You *will* never be sorry.

Part Two

*A young man, recently converted to the Christian faith,
wrote me a letter completely composed of "how to" and "what"
questions. How can I discover God's will for my life? How do
I go about adjusting to old situations as a brand new person?
What can I do to become a better Christian? His letter was a
litany of questions like these.*

*My response to the young man included brief answers to
all the questions he asked. At the conclusion of my letter I added
a word of appreciation to him and remarked that I'd have to
write a book to answer all the questions he raised!*

*You would need a very large book to deal adequately
with all the skills you need for your spiritual pilgrimage. The
second section of this book concerns only a few of the basic ones.
I am firmly convinced that the basic skill for your maturation
as a person of faith is being honest with yourself. You can never
become real apart from that. You also need to know how to
struggle with temptation, how to handle guilt, and how to
discover God's will. Growing up in faith means learning how
to cope with life when things come unglued, and how to learn
from your own experience with Jesus. I discuss each of these
skills in a manner intended to get you moving in the right
direction.*

5

LEARNING TO BE HONEST

YOU HAVE AT LEAST TWO FACES– A FACE you show to the world and a hidden face. The face you show to the world is a fabricated one, composed of behaviors, expressions, words, and impressions you want the world to see. One of the most important questions you must answer for yourself is whether or not the image you project to the world is the real you. Is it the same as your hidden face?

Your hidden face is the real you— your dreams and aspirations as well as your deepest fears and self-doubts. It is made up of your fantasies and hopes and desires and thoughts. Is the face you show to the world consistent with your hidden face? Do you struggle to keep up appearances? Blaise Pascal said that "we strive continually to adorn and preserve our imaginary self, neglecting the true one." If you want to become a real Christian, an authentic person who is fully human and fully alive, you must learn how to include yourself out of Pascal's assertion.

The first step in becoming a genuine Christian is to be yourself before God. This is the simple reason the Bible says that God looks upon our hearts, not our outward appearances. This is why we are cautioned about decorating and pampering our bodies at the expense of becoming real inside (Col. 2:20-23; I Pet. 3:3-4). God is a god of grace. He accepts you for what you are, not what you appear to be. For this reason, the more natural you become before him, the more you drop the projected image and simply be yourself, the more real you become.

Perhaps you will have difficulty removing your public image. Becoming real is harder than taking make-up off your face. It is probably threatening for you to even imagine dropping your outward mask and exposing your naked self. If you did that, people would know what you are really like on the inside, and they might not like what they see. You might even fear that God would slowly shake his head in disapproval. It's safer to wear the public face, to project an image the world will approve. But being safe is not necessarily being real.

The first step in developing your Christian faith, in becoming a real, fully-alive, fully-human being, is simply to be yourself. To do that, you must learn to be honest *with* yourself *about* yourself before God.

Growing out of Phoniness

Fritz Perls, the father of gestalt therapy, defined several levels of neurotic living. He described the first one as "the phony level." This is the level where we live as an *as if* person. An individual lives *as if* he is strong; he lives *as if* he is a big shot; he lives *as if* he is cool; he lives as *if* he is happy; he lives *as if* he is weak; he lives *as if* he is God's gift to the world.

A few years ago an attractive female student with an I.Q. of 150 sat in my office and lamented that very few males would ask her for a date. She believed the young men were intimidated by her intellect. And the only way she knew to cope with this situation was to behave as a nincompoop. So she became one of the campus clowns. She lived *as if* she were a "dumb blond" just to get dates. Like everyone else who lives at the *as if* level, she was a phony.

All of us are phonies at times. You can be a phony in any area of your life— and that especially includes the spiritual one! There are not a few Christians who live *as if*. You can live *as if* you love God when you hate your brother (1 John 4:20). You can live *as if* you have fellowship with God when you really walk in darkness (1 John 1:6). You can live *as if* you have faith when you could care less about others (James 2:14-16). You can live *as if* Jesus is Lord when you refuse to do God's will (Matt. 7:20). You can live *as if* a person is your brother when he is really just a bother. The Bible calls *as if* people hypocrites. They are merely actors, people who wear masks and play parts. Hypocrite is just another word for phony. And a phony isn't real.

You can become a real human being, a genuine disciple, when you recognize your phoniness and start growing out of it. That is why it is so important for you to learn how to be honest with yourself and with God. A person who stays at the *as if* level is a person who has given up on himself. He is a person running away from himself. You actualize your potential for being a fully alive Christian when you stop living and behaving like someone you're not.

E. E. Cummings hit the right note when he wrote: "To be nobody but yourself in a world which is doing its best, night and day, to make you everybody else means to fight the hardest battle any human being can fight." Honesty is your only weapon in this struggle.

Bluffing Causes Sickness

Larry was on the verge of losing his wife and his family when I first met him. He had already lost his church. He was going into his eleventh month as a ministerial dropout. His personal relationships had gone sour. He wasn't cutting it in his new secular job. He was as out of touch with God as he was with himself. Larry's life had come to all this because he never learned to be honest with himself. He got the notion somewhere growing up that men, especially ministers, must play a certain role if they are going to be accepted. There are certain masculine appearances that must be kept at all costs. And so Larry tried to stuff himself into that role. He didn't fit. His inner self shouted that he didn't fit.

Yet Larry didn't know how to deal honestly with his inner voices. He stifled them and played blindman's bluff with his life instead. He kept up the appearances, living *as if* he were someone other than who he really was. At least he kept up appearances until he could no longer afford the emotional payments. The cost of bluffing, of being dishonest, was too high.

The emotional crisis for Larry came just before he resigned his church and the ministry. "I would go into the pulpit on Sundays," he said, "hurting bad inside. I had problems, but I didn't want anyone to know. What I really wanted to do was stand before my congregation and cry. I wanted to tell them how I hurt. But that's the last thing I could do. How would it look for their spiritual leader to have problems? It would be a denial of my faith. So on

Sundays I forced a smile and told them how great it was to be a Christian."

It is great to be a Christian. But it is not a denial of faith to admit that you have problems. Where is it written that God expects you always to be strong and brave and successful and happy and victorious? Where does it say that a Christian is never weak, lonely, fearful, defeated, disillusioned, and a failure? God helps you to cope with life. He does not immunize you against it. Larry had it all backwards. He denied the faith by denying his real feelings. He denied the faith by being one way on the inside and living *as if* he were someone else on the outside. His grand display of faith was all bluff.

Bluffing is a game that comes easy for us because somewhere in growing up we got the idea in our head that we are not acceptable as we are. We learned early that it is dangerous to be honest. So we bluff our way. Rather than admitting our doubts we pretend to believe. Instead of confessing our hurts and failures we pretend everything is cool. We bluff strength when we're weak, assurance when we're insecure, love when we're manipulating, innocence when we're guilty, and courage when we're afraid.

You may not be all that God wants you to be. That's not surprising; we all have some growing up to do. We are all persons-in-process. But bluffing that you are better than you are, or that you are someone different than you really are, is not the way to become a real and healthy person. Bluffing is a road to sickness.

Jesus Valued Honesty

Jesus placed heavy claims upon all who followed him. He demanded radical obedience to his way. Yet Jesus was sensitive enough to know that people do not always live up to expectations. We are not always what we should be.

Jesus also knew that bluffing, being a phony, was not the way to be a real person. He chided the Pharisees because they continued to live at the *as if* stage. Their outward appearance was not a reflection of their inner self. They were like pots clean on the outside and dirty on the inside (Matt. 23:25-26). They were like whitewashed tombs that were full of dead men's bones (Matt. 23:27-28). Jesus could accept people who did not measure up to his demands. He just wanted them to be honest about it!

A distraught father confronted Jesus one day and literally begged him to heal his child (Mark 9:24). Jesus told the man that he would heal the child if the man believed. The father's quick reply was simply, "I believe." Of course he was bluffing, and Jesus knew it. I imagine that Jesus just stood there watching the man in silence. The father, fearful and ashamed, finally muttered something like, "Well, Jesus, to be quite honest, I really don't believe. Please help my unbelief." The man stopped bluffing and became honest about where he was inside his own head. Jesus accepted that. The man did not have the faith Jesus required. Yet he was honest about it, and Jesus healed his child.

On another occasion, Jesus told a story about two men who were praying at the Temple—a tax collector and a Pharisee. The Pharisee spent his time reminding God how good he was. He thought you got close to God by putting on appearances. The tax collector, however, was so overwhelmed by his own sinfulness that he was too embarrassed to look God in the eye. He lowered his head and begged for God's mercy. Jesus said the tax collector went away in step with God. It was not the good man who got close to God; it was the honest man.

Jesus was sitting at Jacob's well, waiting for his disciples to return from the city with food, when a Samaritan woman came to draw water (John 4:7). Jesus struck up a conversation, and before long they were talking about how one finds God. The woman wanted to know if God was in the Samaritan temple on Mt. Gerazim or whether he lived in the Jewish house at Mt. Zion. One of the real tragedies for her is that she was encountering God at Jacob's well in the midst of her daily routine and didn't know it. Jesus told the woman that God was not limited to a plot of real estate. He said that God was a spirit and people could find him only in spirit and truth.

For years I had trouble interpreting that "truth" statement. What did Jesus mean by truth? Was it theological truth? If so, which one of us is really in relationship with God? Very few of us agree on theology. And then one day I saw what Jesus was getting at. It is personal truth, truth about us. Jesus began talking to the woman about her own life. He compelled her to be honest about her own self. She admitted that her life was not virtue incarnate. She was living with a man who was not her husband. So she wasn't what God wanted her to be. When she was honest about herself she became aware of God at the well and her life was changed.

That's what Jesus was talking about when he said that we find God only in spirit and truth. He meant truth about ourselves. You develop a genuine relationship with God when you stop being a phony, when you pull off the mask that disguises the real you. Jesus valued honesty as the way to become a real person.

Risking Honesty with God

The process of dropping our outward masks and being honest about who we really are is always a risky business. Yet it is something God encourages us to do. One who claims to be in step with God but lives contrary to God's ways is a phony (1 John 1:6). One who "walks in the light"— living without secrets, as Bruce Larson puts it— has an authentic relationship with God (1 John 1:7). We are phonies when we cover up our inadequacies (1 John 1:8). But we begin to be real, fully alive Christians when we are honest about ourselves with God: "If we confess our sins, he is faithful and just, and will forgive our sins and cleanse us from all unrighteousness" (1 John 1:9).

You don't have to bluff God about being better than you are. Be honest about your weaknesses as well as your strengths. Be open about the person who is walking around inside your skin. God accepts you for who you really are, not for who you appear to be. You can trust him. He can forgive you and heal you, but only when you are honest about *who* you are and *where* you are on the inside.

I began a week-long Bible conference in Washington, D. C. some years ago by assuring my audience that they could risk being honest with God. I told them he is not some insecure neurotic, that he can take it. He already knows the situation anyway and is simply waiting for us to open up to him so healing can take place. Two days later a woman stopped me after one of the sessions and expressed her appreciation for my words about honesty. Her father had died a month before and she had been angry with God for letting him die. The very thought of feeling that way about God threatened her so much she denied the emotion and buried it deep inside her psyche. She feared that God would reject her for feeling that way. As a result of her bluff, she was unable to cope with her grief and she lost touch with God. After hearing what I said about being honest with God, she risked telling him exactly how she felt. She let it all out—the hurt, the loneliness, the anger she had for God because he let her father die. And you know what? God listened to her. He understood her. He accepted her. From that moment she began working through her grief with the pleasant assurance that God was with her, not against her. The risk of being honest with yourself about yourself before God is worth taking.

After Jesus' death, some of his disciples returned to their fishing business (John 21). They fished all night and caught nothing. Early the next morning they saw a figure standing on shore yelling to them, telling them where fish could be caught. They lowered their nets and caught so many fish the nets began to break. At that moment, someone in the boat recognized that Jesus was the man on the shore. A short while later, all of the disciples were on shore eating some fish that Jesus had prepared. Jesus called Peter aside and asked three times if he loved him more than the boat and nets. Three times Peter responded in the positive. But there was much more to their conversation than comes through in the English translation.

There are several words in the Greek language translated love. The highest word for love is agape. This is the word that is used when the Bible says we are to love God and our neighbor. *Philia* is another word translated "love." But *philia* really means "friendship." With this in mind, let's look again at the conversation between Jesus and Peter.

"Peter, do you have *agape* love for me?

"Lord, I have *friendship* for you!"

"Peter, do you have *agape* for me?"

"Lord, I am your *friend*!"

"Peter, do you really have *friendship* for me?"

"Lord, you *know* I am your friend!"

Peter could have bluffed Jesus. He could have pretended to have the agape that God requires. But he chose to be honest. He risked leveling with Jesus about how he really felt. Jesus did not chide him for not measuring up. He did not condemn him. The biblical text shows that Jesus accepted Peter the way he was and commissioned him into his service.

Jesus will treat you the same way he treated Simon Peter. He will not condemn you for your failures. He will accept you and help you to do better. All he asks is that you be honest with him.

A young boy, thoroughly enculturated by our mass-media world, asked his mother, "Mom, are we live or on tape?" That's a good question for each of us. If you want to grow into a Christian who is fully human and fully alive, a Christian who is real and healthy, develop the art of being honest.

6

WHEN YOUR CONSCIENCE
SAYS YOU'RE BAD

THERE ARE FEW THINGS THAT TAKE the edge off your emotional and spiritual health more than guilt. Huckleberry Finn said that "a bad conscience takes up more room of a fellow's inside than anything else." You have probably already learned that song by heart.

In his book *The Fall*, Albert Camus' main character struggles with the problem of guilt. At one point he confesses, "Well, God's sole usefulness would be to guarantee innocence, and I am inclined to see religion rather as a huge laundry venture— as it was once but briefly, for exactly three years, and it wasn't called religion. Since then, soap has been lacking, our faces are dirty."

Being a real, fully-alive Christian doesn't mean being

sinless. Saints are sinners. Jesus doesn't give you a license to sin, you will claim that right for yourself. You are going to struggle with right and wrong. You're going to get your hands dirty in the process. There will be days when you feel God's judgment. It will be in your head and it is called guilt.

Being a fully alive Christian *does* mean that you know how to deal with your guilt. God has provided some resources for your cleansing. The Christian's faith really is a "laundry venture." And despite Camus' assertion, God's soap is not lacking. You just need to know where to find it. Learning how to handle guilt will help you grow up the way God wants you to.

A Definition of Guilt

Guilt is a feeling of unworthiness that you experience inside. It is the act of reproaching yourself because you do not measure up to certain standards. The guilt you experience can result from some actual fault or from merely contemplating some forbidden behavior. But in either case, guilt is the feeling which results from self-reproach.

Fritz Perl describes guilt as the result of a game we play by ourselves inside ourselves. He calls it the top-dog/under-dog game. One part of you talks to the other part. Top-dog is always beating you over the head with a barrage of shoulds and should-nots —you should be nicer, you should not drive so fast, you should not get angry, you should not eat so much, you should be more interested in God. Underdog is that part of you who is intimidated by Top-dog. Underdog feels guilty; he feels ashamed of himself; he feels beaten down and unworthy.[9]

According to Freudian theory guilt feelings arise from the conflict between your impulses (id) and your conscience (superego). This simply means that your "want-to's" fight your "ought-to's." Hobart Mowrer, another psychologist, on the other hand, believes that guilt results from actual behaviors that contradict your moral standards. There are several theories that attempt to *explain* guilt. But they are relatively unimportant for you unless you are interested in learning how your psychic plumbing works. What is important for you as a person-in-process of becoming fully alive in Jesus is how you *experience* guilt.

There are two kinds of guilt that you experience. They are fake guilt and real guilt. Fake guilt is what you feel when you have done something wrong which is not really wrong in God's eyes. Our parents and society hang taboo signs on numerous behaviors. And in the process of growing up we get the notion that these are God's taboos too. I had a friend in college whose parents taught him that it was a sin to drink cokes. That taboo was indelibly placed on a mental tape he carried around in his head. Consequently, the few times he drank cokes he felt guilty. That's what I call fake guilt. He was violating one of his parent's taboos, but I doubt that God put a checkmark in his sin column. There are many times we experience fake guilt.

Real guilt is just what the name implies. It is guilt feelings that result from doing something the Christian ethic designates a sin. The difficulty for you is that at the feeling level the experience of real and fake guilt is identical. They feel the same. As you mature in your faith, you have the responsibility of distinguishing between the two. Until you learn how to do that both will create problems for you. The secret is knowing how to effectively deal with both.

How Guilt Works

Guilt affects people differently because each person is different. Everyone grows up in his own way. The kind of conscience you develop determines how guilt affects your daily experience. An anti-social person who has a weak conscience lives at odds with the customs and laws of society and feels very little guilt. A person who grows up in a rigid environment may form an excessively strict conscience and feel guilty at the slightest hint of impropriety. The intensity of your guilt feelings depends on a variety of things—the type of conscience you have, the degree of your misconduct, your level of maturity, your sensitivity to ethical values, and your own self-awareness. It's even possible for your guilt feelings to be unconscious. In that event, you can be guilty but not feel guilt at all!

You need to be aware, if you're not already, that your conscience talks to you. St. Paul wrote that real Christian love grows out of a good conscience (I Tim. 1:5). Your conscience, like a weather vane, can change momentarily. It can be either good or bad. A good conscience speaks good things to you. You feel good. A bad conscience scolds you. You feel bad. In either case your conscience is not timid. It talks a lot.

John Drakeford, in his book *Integrity Therapy*, describes the various ways your conscience can express itself. The first is *organ language*. Your conscience can talk to you through physiological functions. Guilt may express itself through a headache, a stomach disorder, or even heart palpitations. There are any number of ways guilt can affect your body.[10]

Your conscience can also use *affective language*. It can speak through your emotions. You can experience guilt as anxiety, depression, fear, bitterness, or some other emotion. Or your conscience may bypass your emotions and use *cognitive language*. Guilt can upset the way you think. You can begin having weird or bizarre thoughts.

Your conscience might speak in *sensory language*. Your senses begin to function in strange ways. You get hacked off at little noises. Your nerves are on edge. People severely troubled by guilt sometimes hear voices that are not there or imagine events that are not real. My favorite bumper sticker is, "You'd be paranoid too if someone were after you!"

A very common way your conscience speaks is through *behavior language*. Sometimes guilt causes compulsive acts like Lady Macbeth's washing the imaginary blood off her hands. Guilt-produced behaviors can also come in milder forms. You may not be able to sleep at night, or you may go out of your way to avoid someone you have wronged. All kinds of behaviors can be launched by guilt. In my college days, while some of my friends were falling in love, my wife-to-be and I struggled into it. We had some fantastic quarrels during our courtship. After those spats my guilt would start churning, causing me to do something to "make it up" to her. She liked the cinnamon twists made in a local bakery. Inevitably, my guilt reaction was to buy a sack of twists and leave them for her at her dorm. She always knew what the sack meant. Any number of behaviors can be prompted by guilt.

Guilt affects people differently. The various

symptoms I've just mentioned are not always the result of guilt, but they can be. Your conscience will speak to you in all kinds of ways. One of the first steps in handling your guilt properly is to be aware of how your conscience speaks to you and be sensitive to what it is saying.

The Value of Guilt

A young mother who was haunted by guilt once came to me for counseling. She felt guilty over almost everything—working outside the home, putting her daughter to bed too late, slacking her duties at work, missing church on Sunday evening, not praying enough, spending too much time in prayer, neglecting her husband. She was almost incapacitated by guilt.

Is guilt all bad, merely creating problems for us as it did for the young mother? Or does guilt serve any good function in our lives? Guilt *can* be a positive factor in our emotional and spiritual health. In itself, guilt is neither good nor bad. But it can become either. It is like a red warning light on the dashboard of your car.

If the temperature light comes on in your car, a good purpose is served. You immediately know there is trouble under the hood. The same is true if the oil light flickers. If the lights come on and you ignore them, you're in for trouble. Guilt works the same way in your life. It is a red light on your mental dashboard. When you become aware of guilt feelings, ask yourself why. The pressure of guilt feelings means something is not working right inside. If you use the cue to discover what is wrong and correct it, guilt has served a good purpose. If you ignore the guilt and handle it in an inadequate fashion, you're in for trouble. But how do you handle guilt appropriately?

How to Handle Guilt

Paul Tournier, in *The Person Reborn*, reminds us that our task as Christians is not to avoid mistakes so much as it is to be fruitful. We are to create good out of evil. As he so aptly puts it, "if we try to build good out of good, we are in danger of running out of raw material."[11]

So you misbehave and feel guilty about it. There are several practical things you can do to bring good out of your evil. The first step is to *accept your guilt*. Those who work with alcoholics know that such persons can be helped only when they are willing to admit their drinking problem and ask for help. The same is true of other drug abusers, compulsive gamblers, or even those who struggle with obesity. It seems to be a principle of nature that we can begin to cope with a problem only when we admit the problem.

When you suffer guilt admit it. Accept

responsibility for its cause. Don't blame others. You can handle the guilt only when you stop denying it, avoiding it, rationalizing it, forgetting about it, or thinking it will go away. So put away all your excuses and accept the guilt.

Second, *confess your guilt*. For best results confession should take two directions. You should confess whatever has caused your guilt to God. The Bible assures you that God will hear your prayers *grace*fully. When you admit your misbehavior to him he is faithful to forgive [your] sins and cleanse from all unrighteousness" (1 John 1:9). There are three things important in this promise. Notice the word *all*. That's a small word, but it includes every possible sin. God will cleanse any sin you commit. The verbs *forgive* and *cleanse* are in the present tense in the Greek text. This means that God continues to cleanse you. As long as you confess, there is no end to his mercy. And finally, the word translated "forgive" is the Greek verb for "divorce." When you confess your sins to God, he heals you by divorcing you from what you have down.

To deal adequately with guilt, you also need to confess your sin to a significant other. I know this takes guts to do, but many people carry unresolved guilt around in their head like excess baggage even *after* they have confessed to God. And the reason is they have not confessed their sin to another. Sometimes the other person should be the person you have sinned against. This is not, however, always the wisest thing to do. It depends on the sin. To confess to a friend you have lied about him is one thing. To disclose an act of marriage infidelity to your spouse is quite another. That kind of confession leads to other complications. So in some instances your confessions should be made to an intimate friend, a minister, or a counselor. But whatever you confess, the confessor should be someone who is significant to you and someone whom you trust

The reason it is important for you to confess to another is so God can mediate his forgiveness to you. God works through people. When you feel guilty you also feel alienated from others and ashamed. When a significant other hears your confession and then accepts you, the feeling of alienation vanishes. You can more easily realize God's acceptance when you experience acceptance from others. This is why the Bible says, "Confess your sins to one another and be healed" (James 5:16).

Third, *make restoration for your guilt.* At the college where I am employed, there is a five dollar bill and a typed note scotch-taped to a glass case in the bookstore. Both are from a former student. The note is a confession that as a student he (or she) stole an item from the store. The five dollars more than covered the price of the article. Guilt finally caught up with that person. And he or she handled it by making restitution.

There are some deeds for which restitution cannot be made. But if your guilt-producing behavior can be rectified, do it. This is a point where you need to be sensitive to your intuition. How often has someone wanted to "make it up to you" when they have mistreated you in some way? God has built that natural inclination into us. Repair the damage if you can. Do you remember how Zacchaeus handled his guilt after he met Jesus (Luke 19:8)? He repaid the taxes he had collected illegally with interest and gave half of everything he owned to the poor.

Fourth, *learn from your guilt*. George Santayana said that those who do not know the past are doomed to repeat it. Federick Hegel, a nineteenth century philosopher, wrote that the only thing we learn from history is that we don't learn from history. The observation of both men can be correct. It depends upon the person. You do have the ability to learn from your past. And your guilt can help. The things that cause you to feel guilt are areas where you perhaps need to do some work on yourself. If particular behaviors create problems for you and inhibit meaningful relationships with God and others, you have a cue as to where and how you need to modify your actions.

As you mature into a real and fully-alive Christian, you will become more sensitive to God's will and your own inabilities to measure up to his standards. Consequently, your struggle with guilt will be a continual one. Your struggle can move in either of two directions. You can struggle unto life, or you can struggle unto death. Appropriate handling of guilt is a struggle unto life— real life!

7

HOW TO HANDLE
TEMPTATION

ONE DAY WHILE MY WIFE AND I were discussing the nature
of commitment, she made an offhand comment which
seems more profound every time I think of it: "You can
never make a one-time commitment that lasts forever."
That is a very subtle bit of wisdom.

The observation is true about marriage. On June 26,
1959, Carolyn and I stood at the altar and exchanged our
marriage vows. We pledged ourselves to each other. Today,
if anyone should ask us when we were married we would
point back to that time and place. But that is not when we
were married at all That's when we began to be married.
Marriage is a process. The vows we took at the altar do not
carry us through "better or worse until death parts us." If
either of us desires to keep the marriage vows, we must

make them again in our minds every time we are tempted to break them. A vow given at one time does not automatically last forever.

A commitment once made must be remade continually as long as you wish it to be valid. If you vow today that you will diet for the next ten days, today's vow doesn't carry you through. You must recommit yourself to that vow every time you are tempted to take a few calories on the side. An alcoholic knows that he must renew his vow of abstinence every time he is tempted to drink. One pledge given the day he jumps "on the wagon" doesn't last the rest of his life. The reason so many New Year's resolutions are never kept is because they are made on New Year's Day. One vow does not have the staying power to carry you through the entire year any more than the food you eat today has enough nutrition to fuel your body tomorrow. It is a profound insight indeed. A commitment that lasts a lifetime cannot be made once.

Your commitment to follow Jesus is like any other vow. You have surrendered yourself to him, and pledged yourself to do his will. Your commitment is commendable. Yet it won't last the rest of your spiritual pilgrimage. If you remain faithful to him, you must reaffirm your loyalty every time you are tempted to go astray. This doesn't mean that you cease being his disciple when you sin, anymore than a marriage is automatically dissolved when one of the spouses is not true to the marriage vows. It merely underlines the fact that life with Jesus is a vital, dynamic, and growing relationship. The relationship is strengthened and enriched when you are true to your vows. It is weakened when you fail to keep your commitment up to date. This is why the Bible says the just live each day by faith (Heb. 2:44). The faith required the day you were converted is necessary each day of your pilgrimage. The day you first committed yourself to Jesus is not the day you were saved. It is the day you *began* to be saved.

All of this is to say that your growth as a Christian hinges upon how you respond to temptation. You will be tempted every day to betray your vows to God. You will yield to many of the temptations. You will sin. A child stumbles a lot when he's learning to walk. This does not mean, however, that you are to go on sinning as you did before. Growing up in the faith means acting more responsibly before God and others. You become a more mature Christian as you learn how to handle temptation.

Discovering the Right

I sat in rapt attention as an old Filipino told us some of his experiences during World War II. He lived in a small barrio north of Manila in those days. When the Japanese first began to infiltrate the island the Americans retreated, and in the process some of the American soldiers got separated from their units. One such soldier appeared at the old gentleman's village. The old man and a few others hid him in a nearby cave and kept him supplied with food. When the Japanese came they lined all of the villagers before a machine gun and asked, among other things, if they knew where any Americans were hiding. The old man paused, looked at me, and asked, "What was I to do? The Bible tells me not to lie. But if I had told them what they asked, the soldier would have been killed."

Making decisions about right and wrong is easy when you have a choice between white and black. The Bible identifies some behaviors which you always know are right or wrong. But how do you put your finger on what is right when you're dealing with shades of gray, when it is not clear which fork of the moral road you follow?

Jesus taught that a gray area behavior is right when it conforms to three principles—*kawwahah, lishmah*, and *agape*. The word *kawwanah* refers to intention, or motive. You cannot always judge a behavior by its cover—it's outward appearance— any more than you can judge a book that way. A behavior must be assessed in light of what intention motivates it. If I slapped you in the face, for example, would that be a good act or a bad act? It depends upon my motive. If my behavior is prompted by hostility, it is wrong. But what if you are hysterical, or have taken an overdose of pills, and I am trying to bring you back to a level of consciousness? Slapping you in the face is the same in either case, but my motives for doing so would color its meaning.

What motivates your behavior? Are your motives self-serving? Do your motives reflect the character of Jesus? When you want to determine whether a behavior is right, take a peek beneath its cover to see what motivates it. An act is only as good as its motive.

The word *lishmah* is best translated "for its own sake." It refers to doing a particular act just because it is right. Jesus taught that a person could perform an apparently good act, like praying, giving charity, or fasting, but if he did such things for some purpose other than that they are right in themselves, they are wrong (Matt. 6:1-18).

I once belonged to a church whose members were encouraged to pay their financial pledges before the end of December. Only one reason was given—pay so you can deduct it from your income tax. We were asked to give in order to benefit ourselves. Giving had an ulterior purpose; it was not done for its own sake. No one ever told us that if we promised a certain amount to the church we ought to fulfill our pledge just because it was the right thing to do. A good act is performed just because it is right.

Jesus also taught that good behavior is consistent with *agape*, or love (Luke 6:27-36). This word for love does not refer to an emotional feeling. It designates a way of behaving. Love is something you do. It means to do what is best for the other person in a situation instead of what is best for yourself. This is why you can love your enemies (Luke 6:27). You don't have to like a person to treat him in the right way. God behaves *agape* towards you (John 3:16). You are to model his behavior towards others (1 John 3:16). An act is good if it is consistent with *agape*.

Determining the Right

T. B. Maston and William Pinson, Jr.[12] offer some practical suggestions that might help you determine what is right. They list three questions and three tests for determining right from wrong in the gray areas.

When you are struggling with a moral problem, or a temptation to do something you're not quite sure is right, there are three questions that may help you in determining what you ought to do. The first question is, "What effect will this behavior have on me?" How will your participation in the act affect your body, your mind, your health, your self-image? A second question is, "How will my participation in this affect others?" Will the behavior in question strengthen others or weaken others? And a third question is, "How will this act affect the cause of Christ?" As a Christian, you are involved in a movement. You are not a lone-ranger Christian. Will the behavior in question increase or decrease your influence for good in your little corner of the world? Negative answers to these three questions may indicate the proposed action is wrong for you.

There are also three tests you can apply to help determine whether an act is right or wrong. The first is a test of secrecy. Are there persons you would not want to know you are doing this? Would you mind if your best friend, parent, or pastor knew about it? The second test is one of universality. What if everybody did this? How would it affect society? What kind of family or church would we have if everyone did this? And a third test is one of prayer. Can you ask God's approval for what you propose to do? Would God grant his blessing? Again, negative answers to these tests may indicate that the behavior in question may not help you mature in your faith.

Your Decisions Are Important

The choices you make with reference to good and bad behavior are most important. This is because your decisions shape the person you become. Who you are is determined by your genetic inheritance, your environment, and the decisions you make. And the only one you control today is the latter.

Compare yourself with a wooden desk. You both exist. Yet you, as a human being, exist in a different way. The desk cannot determine itself. It has no will of its own, certainly no free will. Whatever the desk is has been determined by forces outside itself. Someone else has determined that the wood would be a desk. Someone else has determined its size, shape, and color. Everything about it has been fashioned by forces outside of itself.

You have potential to exist at a different level. I say potential because the choice is yours. It doesn't happen automatically. If you are determined by forces outside yourself, your existence is in no way different from the desk. If your values, morals, beliefs, ideas, manner of dress, or behavior is determined by others, you have abdicated the one potential that makes you human—-the right to determine yourself, the right to choose and make decisions. When you accept responsibility for yourself and decide for yourself how you will live, you will become an authentic person.

The decisions you make for yourself shape you. If you choose to do the good you will become good; if you decide to behave honestly you will become honest; if you decide to act lovingly you will become loving. How you behave shapes who you become. It is very important that you learn to make the right choices in moral and ethical matters. For how you choose to live today affects who you become tomorrow.

Facing Temptation

It is a fact of life that *knowing* the right is not the same as *doing* the right. As you grow in the faith your sensitivity to what is right and wrong will sharpen. And this will parallel your struggle with temptation. For as long as you live you will always be tempted. Your maturity as a Christian will depend in part on how you handle temptation. You remain a phony as long as you claim to follow Jesus but let your temptations push you around. You grow into a mature Christian as you learn to master your temptations.

The first step in handling temptation is to let it be. Temptation is not a sin. It is an invitation to sin. Realize first of all that you are not sinning when you are tempted. Jesus was tempted severely, yet he was not a sinner (Heb. 4:1-5). When you are tempted, simply let the temptation be. This is what the Bible means when it says to "resist the devil and he will flee from you" (James 4:7). The more you struggle with a temptation, or try to run away from it, the more of a problem it becomes. Don't act on your temptation. Just let it lie there. After a while, it will go away.

I read the story of a reformed alcoholic who was really struggling with the temptation to drink again. On his way to the corner bar he passed his minister's house. He saw a light and went to the door. As the minister greeted him the trembling alcoholic said, "Preacher, if I don't get a drink I'm going to die." The minister blurted out, "Sam, go home and die!" The next morning Sam was back. He had a smile on his face as big as a rainbow as he said to his minister, "Reverend, I just wanted you to know I died last night!" That's letting it be.

A second way of handling temptation is to accept responsibility for the temptation. Some people put the blame on God for their temptations. But God isn't the source (James 1:13). Others try to hang it on the devil—"the devil made me do it!" Yet although the Bible says we are tempted by the devil we cannot excuse ourselves by sticking our tongues out at him. Adam and Eve tried that in the garden, but it didn't work.

To cope effectively with temptation you must accept responsibility for it. For the temptation grows out of your own lusts and desires (James 1:15). Because this is so, your temptations can be a clue as to what areas in your life you need to work on. They may indicate situations or behavior for which you need to find resources to help you cope. Jesus once said that if your hand or eye or foot causes you to sin, or keeps you from doing God's will, you ought to rid yourself of it. That's picture-talk for accepting responsibility for your own behavior. No one causes you to behave a certain way. You choose how you act. You are in charge of you. Don't abdicate your potential of self-determination to your temptations or other forces outside yourself.

A third way to handle temptation is to develop God confidence. God will help you in your struggle to live on the right side: "No temptation has overtaken you that is not common to man. God is faithful, and he will not let you be tempted beyond your strength, but with the temptation will also provide the way of escape, that you may be able to endure it" (1 Cor. 10:13). This statement includes three promises to you from God regarding your temptations. The first is that your temptations are "common to man." You are not lured away from the right path with temptations designed to snare a god. Your temptations are human. So you battle on equal terms.

The promise also affirms that God will not let you face more than you can handle. You are not alone in your struggle. God can he involved with you if you move over and give him room. This promise abolishes any excuses you might have about your temptations being stronger than you can bear. It also offers hope that you can overcome whatever tempts you.

And notice that God always offers a way out with each temptation you face. This does not mean that victory over evil is easy. It does not mean that God's way is escapism, a running away from life. The "way of escape" is identified in the last phrase of the biblical promise. It is endurance. That is the escape God was talking about. If you develop confidence in God's ability to help you live life, if you open your life to him instead of going it alone, he will help you bear up under temptation. You will not be crushed by it.

And When You Don't

To be quite candid, you will not always conquer your temptations. You will sin. Sometimes you will sin because you are in a situation where nothing seems right and you have to do the next best thing. This is what Martin Luther meant by "sinning bravely." Sometimes you will sin because you cannot see well enough in the gray area to distinguish the good from the bad. Sometimes you will sin unintentionally, you will merely slip up. But most of the time you probably will sin just because you want to. You know the right but you desire the wrong. What do you do when you don't handle your temptations very well? You do the same thing you did when you were converted. You trust in God's grace. You confess your sins to him and accept his forgiveness,

Karl Menninger, in *The Vital Balance*,[13] recounts a story of Thomas Jefferson. The President and some companions were riding horseback cross-country. They were obliged to ford a swollen stream. A traveler on foot waited at the water's edge until several of the party crossed, and then asked the President to help him across. Jefferson took him upon the back of his horse and carried him across the stream. On the other side, one of the men asked, "Tell me, why did you select the President to ask for this favor?" The man answered, "I didn't know he was the President. All I know is that on some faces is written the answer 'no' and on some the answer 'yes.' His face was one of the latter."

God has a yes-face. When you confess your sins to him he is faithful to forgive you. He will put your sins out of reach: "As far as the east is from the west, so far does he remove our transgressions from us" (Ps. 103:12). He will put your sins out of sight: "Blessed is he whose transgression is forgiven, whose sin is covered" (Ps. 32:1). And he will put your sins out of mind: "I will forgive their iniquity, and I will remember their sin no more" (Jer. 31:34).

8

STAYING ON TOP
WHEN THE BOTTOM FALLS
OUT

EVELYN UNDERHILL, A PROMINENT BRITISH theologian, has said that sooner or later everyone in the Christian life goes on the night shift. Can you imagine what she meant by that? When a person goes on the night shift his whole routine is altered—schedule, habits, attitudes, desires, and body adjustments. The night shift drastically changes one's style.

I once heard a radio preacher say that a person would never suffer if he would go to church, pray regularly, read the Bible, and tithe. I wonder how he explained Jesus? He did God's will perfectly, and all he got was a cross. Paul was a rather obedient Christian. Yet he almost spent more time in jail than out. You can put it down in your notebook with large print—CHRISTIANS SUFFER. As you follow Jesus on your journey to become a real, fully-alive person, there will be many times you have to go on the night shift. You will experience moments when there are no hallelujahs to be sung. There will be times your whole existence will ache with sorrow and life will be no fun at all.

One day, while browsing through a bookstore, I was impressed with how many self-help books there were. There are tons of words in print advising us how to be happy, solve our problems, and live essentially worry-free lives. Those books are fine. But what we really need are some more words telling us how to cry. For you, even as a Christian, are going to spend a sizeable part of your life doing just that. There is no way for you to *escape* suffering, so you need to know how to *experience* it. To grow and mature as a Christian, you need to develop a theology of hurt. Perhaps this chapter will help you get that assignment under way.

Suffering and the Scheme of Things

Perhaps the first lesson you can learn as you develop your theology of hurt is that suffering is a part of the scheme of things in our world. There is no such thing as a stick with only one end. Look around the next time you are outside. You will see that every stick has at least two ends. And that's the way it is with life. We always experience life as polarity. Every up has a down; every in has an out; every fast has a slow; every front has a back; every pleasure has a pain. The world we were told about in the fairy tales— where people marry and live happily ever after—is a Hollywood set. It is a fabricated place that only exists in our imaginations. There is no pain-free existence; suffering is part of the fabric from which life is cut. Death is real. People are hungry. Marriages fall apart. Friendships disintegrate. Dreams evaporate. Hope vanishes. People reject each other. People fight each other. Children run away from home. Families don't speak. The bottom falls out and people don't know why. But they do hurt. And the hurt is as painful as any physical pain they can experience. Hurt can stoop a person's shoulders and buckle his knees. Suffering is part of the scheme of things.

A psalmist in ancient Israel once sang: "My heart is in anguish within me, the terrors of death have fallen upon me. Fear and trembling come upon me, and horror overwhelms me, And I say, 'Oh that I had wings like a dove! I would fly away and be at rest'" (Ps. 55:4-6).

Dove's wings are what some people want when they run up against suffering. They want to run out on life. They want to cope with life by copping out of life. I understand how they feel. Sometimes I get so burdened under the load my impulse is to run away. But run where? Does life have those places where we can be "home free," where suffering can't touch us?

I call the impulse to run away from life the "Jonah Complex." And it is not an uncommon disease! A young man, finding himself increasingly unable to cope with mounting problems at home, at work, and with his parents, told me not long ago that he was going to walk off one morning and never come back. He would tell no one *that* he was going; he would tell no one *where* he was going; he was just going. He had the Jonah Complex.

There will be moments when you too will feel like running. Perhaps you will want to run away from responsibilities, or difficulties, or hell at home, or a spouse, or a parent, or even God. Life will lay some heavy burdens on you at times. You will long for dove's wings. Your suffering may be so intense at times that you will see no way out except to run. Yet that is an illusion. One of the greatest sources of pain is trying to avoid pain. To cope with suffering, you must never turn your back on life. There is really no place to go. You have to learn how to make peace where you are. The first step in learning how to suffer is to accept it.

Find a Purpose

Once you have accepted suffering, you can cope if you find a purpose in it. Suffering is no barrel of laughs, but it can be a means of growth and maturity for you. As T. B. Maston, a beloved acquaintance of mine, has said, suffering can make you *bitter* or it can make you *better*.

Victor Frankl, one of the foremost psychiatrists in this century, survived the Nazi concentration camps during World War II. His experience gave him insight into what makes humans tick. He discovered that one matures and grows healthier when he can find meaning in his suffering: "To live is to suffer, to survive is to find meaning in the suffering. If there is a purpose in life at all, there must be a purpose in suffering and dying. But no man can tell another what this purpose is. Each must find out for himself, and must accept the responsibility that his answer prescribes. If he succeeds he will continue to grow in spite of all indignities."[14]

Simon Peter played the same tune when he wrote to first century Christians who were trying to cope with religious persecution from the government. He likened suffering to smelting furnaces (1 Pet. 1:6-7). In his day, gold ore was put into furnaces which in turn were raised to a very high temperature. The heat would cause all the impurities in the ore to rise to the top. The impurities would be skimmed off, leaving pure gold. The Bible teaches that suffering can do the same for your faith. When you cope with suffering in the proper way, your faith comes out stronger; it is purified like gold.

I have found that the first question many people ask when they suffer is "why?" "What have I done to deserve this?" "Why me, Lord?" Of course, "why" is not a profitable question. For in reality no one ever really knows why. We can only guess. You may recall that this was one of Jesus' final words from the cross: "My God, why have you forsaken me?" You will also notice that there was no answer.

The question we need to ask if we are to find meaning, or purpose, in our suffering is "What?" God speaks to us through all of life's experiences. There are things we can learn through suffering which we cannot learn any other way—-important things like sensitivity to others, empathy, kindness, and concern. When you suffer, substitute what for why. What is God saying to me through this? When you find an answer to that question you have discovered the purpose in your suffering.

Acknowledge God's Concern

The next step in coping with suffering is to acknowledge God's concern for your plight. Contrary to popular opinion, God does not cause suffering. He does not rejoice when people suffer. What happens to you matters to God. He cares for you (1 Pet. 5:7).

A young deacon in a church had a promising future. His business was going well. His marriage was working. His family enjoyed the material amenities that accompany success. He was happy. He was a leader in his church. God was good to him, and he had the world by the tail. But then Halloween came. His daughter's costume caught fire while she was out trick-or-treating, and she burned to death. The father could not cope well with the tragedy. He blamed God and vowed never to call upon him again. In the succeeding months he became an embittered hermit, isolating himself from everyone who could help him bear the tragedy.

A number of people get the idea that God causes suffering. How can God be all-loving and all-powerful at the same time? If he is all-powerful and does nothing to prevent suffering, he is not loving. And if he wants to prevent suffering but cannot, he is not powerful. The apparent contradiction makes for enlivened discussions in the classroom. Yet it seldom touches where we hurt.

God does not rejoice in your hurting any more than you do. Why then does he permit it? I don't have an answer for that. But I do know that there are parents who try to raise their children in an incubation ward. They try to protect them from all dangers and in the process overprotect them. What kind of person does an overprotected child become? What does he grow up to be when his parents use their money and influence to always bail him out of difficulties? Perhaps God doesn't immunize us against life because he doesn't want us to grow up distorted.

God does not *cause* suffering. There are too many letters in that word. Subtract the *ca*: God *uses* suffering. God never tests man with evil (James 1:13). Your suffering is God's suffering. He's not enjoying heavenly bliss while you have to go it alone.

God suffers too. He really cares about what happens to you. You can better cope with your problems if you acknowledge his concern.

Accept God's Help

Another step in coping with suffering is to accept God's help. God doesn't keep you from life's suffering, but neither does he abandon you to life. God helps you bear up under life without being crushed by it.

The Bible strongly affirms that God can help you cope with life: "In everything God works for good with those who love him" (Rom. 8:28). The original text does not say that "all things work for good." You know better than that. Everything that happens to you is *not* good. This promise asserts that *God* works in all things, no matter how bad they are, for your good.

St. Paul wrote that he could do all things through Christ who strengthened him (Phil. 4:13). Paul was not a guru who lived on a mountaintop above all suffering and pain. This statement comes on the heels of his confession that he was experiencing all of life's ups and downs. The phrase "I can *do* all things" literally means "I can *endure* all things." Jesus offers you endurance to cope, not to cop.

The writer of Hebrews reminded his readers that Jesus knew what it was to suffer. Life was no bowl of cherries for him. And for that very reason he is able to empathize with us in our hurts. We can come to him with confidence that he offers us grace to help us in our times of need (Heb. 4:14-16).

An acquaintance of mine and I were on our way to lunch when he told me his story. Ed has an important and prestigious position with one of the largest denominations in this country. He had spent his entire ministry in California before assuming his present post. His new job was in another state, but he felt the move was God's will. So he and his wife pulled up their roots and resettled. Six months after moving to the new position, Ed went for a checkup. His doctor dealt him a stunning blow. He had leukemia and about six months to live. Ed returned to some specialists in California to get a second opinion. Their story was the same. He had about six months.

Ed handled this news like most other people—badly. He wouldn't believe it. He fought against it. And he grew very bitter. He was especially angry with God. After all, God knew he was going to get leukemia. Why did he let him leave his work and friends in California for this new job? Why did he add the agony of readjusting to moving when he must begin adjusting to dying? Ed was sinking and he knew it. As a minister he had helped countless others walk through death, but he didn't know how to die.

One morning Ed sat on his bed and talked straight with himself. He could go on chafing the way he was doing and die a thousand times in the next six months. Or he could reaffirm life, live one day at a time trusting in God, and at the end of the six months die only once. He opted for the latter. He said to me later: "I began to take each day as it came, living one day at a time. I lived each day trusting in God instead of fighting God. And I've been doing that for eleven years!"

I am not saying that, if you will live by faith, God will give you eleven years, six months, or one week. Ed's experience does not mean that trust in God automatically solves all your problems and erases all your suffering. What I am saying is that you can learn what Ed discovered. God can help you cope!

I have already mentioned that you can cope with life by asking *what* instead of *why*. Another question that helps you cope is *who*. The healthy question is not "*why* is this happening to me?" but "*who* is with me in this suffering?"

A little boy is happily playing in the basement, oblivious to the world about him and to a storm that is raging outside.

All of a sudden the lights go out. The room is totally black. The child is shocked into consciousness from his play. And for a moment he stands there afraid, not knowing where to move, because it's dark. Then he hears footsteps outside the door. Anxiety grips his stomach. He becomes more frightened as the steps get closer. His heart begins to race. He hears a hand fumbling for the doorknob and anxiety overwhelms him as he almost sees those imaginary goblins. The door opens, and he hears the voice out of the darkness. "Alan? Are you in here? Are you all right?" The boy sighs with relief. The anxiety vanishes. He breathes again. He can handle it. Oh, the darkness is still there. The cause of his fear still surrounds him. But now he can cope with it. His daddy is there with him. And that makes all the difference in the world.

As you grow in your faith, you will have to come to terms with suffering. You will wonder sometimes whether you get more than your share. You will question whether God knows you hurt or whether he cares. You might even be tempted to run out on him because he doesn't snap his fingers and make your troubles go away. But remember that how you struggle will determine how you grow. Suffering can make you better. You can grow through suffering. You can handle it and become more real, more alive, in the process if you accept it, find a purpose in it, acknowledge God's concern, and accept his help. Ask *who*. For when the lights go out and you're afraid, your Daddy's there. And that makes a difference!

9

FINDING GOD'S WILL

IN A MEMORABLE SCENE FROM MARC Connolly's play, *The Green Pastures*, Moses announces that he has given Joshua the responsibility of leading Israel. Moses had stood before an angry Pharaoh. He had pushed on when others wanted to quit. He had believed in God when others doubted. But now, in spite of all that, God had forbidden him to enter the Promised Land. In the play, someone asks Moses why God is treating him this way. Moses' reply is, "God has got plans for me."

You can be certain that God has some plans for you, just as he had for Moses. St. Paul prayed that the new Christians at Colossae might "be filled with the knowledge of his will in all spiritual wisdom and understanding" (Col. 1:9). Every one of us needs that too, if we are going to mature in Christ. The phrase, "knowledge of his will" means to have special insight into what God wants. The terms "spiritual wisdom and understanding" are used frequently in the New Testament for the ability to apply knowledge in practical situations. Salvation involves growth in understanding what God's will is for your life and how it may be implemented in your everyday circumstances.

God has given you a new life in Jesus. Now you must decide what you are going to do with it. Jose Ortega y Gasset in *What is Philosophy?* defines man as a being who consists not so much in what he is as in what he is going to be.

The person you become tomorrow hinges upon how you respond to God's plans for you today. Your potentiality can become actuality—-you can become real—only as you learn to know and do God's will.

Defining God's Will

One day when Albert Schweitzer was a professor of philosophy, he began tidying up his cluttered desk so he could prepare his next lecture. As he picked up papers to either discard or place somewhere else, he laid his hands on a magazine published by the Paris Missionary Society. He was about to throw it in the wastebasket when an article entitled "The Needs of the Congo Mission" caught his eye. Schweitzer read the entire article before putting it down.

That night he wrote in his diary, "My search is over." The rest of his story is modern legend.

Albert Schweitzer is not the only Christian ever to invest his life doing what he considered to be God's will. Every real Christian does that. The heroes of our faith, men like Abraham, Jacob, David, Peter, and Paul, did not become great men because of their goodness, or intellectual wit, or abilities. They were all quite ordinary persons, with weaknesses and faults like everybody else. Their greatness was in the kind of relationship they had with God. Each one of them was willing to risk himself in doing God's will. Spiritual growth always involves that kind of risk.

The concept of God's will is interpreted in a wide variety of ways by Christians. There are those who believe that God determines everything that happens. They consider all of life to be his will. As a minister, I have heard numerous persons respond to tragedy with something like, "Well, I don't understand why God let this happen, but someday I will." It is a common idea that "whatever will be will be" is God's will."

There is also a mechanistic view that the only plan God has for the world is to let the world be. He created it to work by certain natural laws, and he lets it work that way. He never interferes.

Still others believe that God has a will for everyone's

life, but that he does not force that will upon anyone. A person must freely choose it. According to this view, God does not will everything to happen that does happen, but he does permit it because he gives man the freedom to determine his own life. And that means that man must be responsible to accept the consequences of his actions.

Of course, these are not the only three ways God's will is understood by Christians. And even within these three major concepts there are all kinds of modified viewpoints. It can get confusing. What *is* God's will? Does he have a script in heaven with your name on it—a script that mentions the vocation you should follow, whom you should marry, where you should live, and when you should move there? Martin Luther and John Calvin reacted against church practice in the sixteenth century by declaring that God's will includes everyone's station in life, not just the clergy. And so we have the current idea that God calls people to be doctors, lawyers, and janitors, as well as he calls ministers and missionaries. Does God's will for your life include specifics such as these? If so, how many specifics of your daily life are included? I know a person who seeks God's will before making any decision, whether that decision concerns buying a new car or taking the family on vacation. What is God's will? If you are going to live by it, you must first know how to define it.

The biblical phrase translated "God's will" literally

means "God's wish." The Bible nowhere explicitly says that God has an ironclad will for every decision you make in life. There may be occasions when his will is specific about what you do or where you go, yet the Bible does not say that God has a complete itinerary for your journey. He does, however, have a wish for how you live.

I remember one occasion not long ago when my youngest daughter had difficulty making a decision. Each of her two close friends—Whitney and Kelly—had invited her over to play. Kym couldn't make up her mind which invitation to accept, After a while she asked me which she should choose. "I don't care," I responded. "You may visit whomever you want. But wherever you go, I expect you to behave."

I have discovered in my own experience that God's will works much the same way. There are times his will is definite. God wants us to do a particular thing. At other times he leaves the decision to us. He wants us to follow our own interests and use our own minds in making the decision. But God never wants us to act out of character as his children. His wish is that our values, behavior, desires, and decisions reflect his character. His will always includes the "I expect you to behave" clause. God's will for you is his wish that you find meaning in your life and mind your manners in the process.

Describing God's Will

There are many statements that describe God's will. One of them is that *God's will is always best for you.* This does not mean that you will have a trouble-free existence if you do his will. It does not imply that life inside God's will is easier than life outside it. Jesus uttered "thy will be done" while he was in agony, and sometimes you too will speak those words when your life is falling apart. To say that God's will is best for you means that God is never working against you in life. His will is always designed with your best interests at heart.

The Apostle Paul once wrote that God's will is good, acceptable, and perfect (Rom. 12:2). The word *good* means morally good. We use the word in this sense when we describe someone as being a good person. The word *acceptable* should be translated *right*. It means that God's will for you is always headed in the right direction. His will can enliven and embellish you as a person. God's will never diminishes you. The word *perfect* is best translated "complete." It means here to be spiritually mature. God's will is always best for you because it moves you towards that which gives meaning and wholeness to your existence.

God's will for you is always behavioral. As you read the Bible you will discover that his will is never referred to as some intellectual glob that you are to contemplate. It is not a subject for philosophical musing. God's will is practical. It is down-to-earth. It touches life where you live and it always concerns how you behave. Jesus frequently spoke of doing God's will (Matt. 7:21). Paul assured some immature Christians in Thessalonica, who thought God could care less about their sexual practices, that God's will for them was to behave morally (1 Thess. 4:3), He also reminded them that God wished for them to behave in a decent manner towards each other (1 Thess. 5:12-22). Even James encouraged his readers to live by God's will instead of their own wants (James 4:13-17). God's will is his wish for your behavior to mirror his character in everything you do.

God's will is personal. When I began my pilgrimage with Jesus, I tried my best to mimic other Christians I knew and respected. Their beliefs became my beliefs; their religious practices became my practices. I started out trying to be someone else. And it was like putting on another person's clothes which are several sizes too small. My spiritual life was uncomfortable. Deep inside I knew that I was not real. The mask I wore to church wasn't the real me. Sometimes I doubted the genuineness of my own salvation. As I listened to other Christians tell what they had experienced in God. I knew my experience was different from theirs, and automatically assumed that theirs was real and mine was counterfeit. I struggled this way for several years until I realized that each person experiences God in his own way. God does not make us all alike. We each have different spiritual fingerprints. He affirms our own individuality. God does not want carbon-copy Christians. He wants us to be ourselves. That's why he has given each of us different gifts (Rom. 12:6). His will is that we use our gifts in ministering to each other (Rom. 12:4-8). God's will for you is designed especially for you.

God's will is slanted in your direction. Some years ago I listened to an evangelist warn his audience that God would kill their children, break their arms, or strike them with some dread disease unless they did his will. That is certainly not consistent with the God Jesus revealed. God cares for you. You are free to choose or reject his will for your life, but in any case he works for your good. God is not lined up against you. His will is slanted in your direction. It is in your best interest. This is why the Bible says that God is working in all things, even the bad experiences, for your good (Rom. 8:28). Sometimes you will find it difficult to see God working in your life, but you can trust in the fact that his will for you is good.

A Chinese philosopher once told a parable about an old man and his son who lived in an abandoned fort. One day the only horse the old man owned wandered away, and his neighbors came by to express their sorrow over his misfortune. "How do you know it is ill-fortune?" he asked. A week later his horse returned leading a herd of wild horses. The old man's friends exulted in his good fortune. "How do you know that it is good?" the man responded. Soon after that his son started to ride one of the horses, but fell off and broke his leg. The neighbors again expressed their sorrow. "How do you know it is bad?" the man asked. The following week a Chinese war lord came through the village conscripting young men for battle. He would not take the old man's son because of his broken leg. The neighbors rejoiced over this favorable turn of events, "How do you know that it is favorable?" said the old man.

The parable ends there, but the point is clear. We cannot judge whether or not something is good for us until life is over. Each experience must be judged in light of our whole existence. Have you ever experienced something you thought was very bad? At the time you would almost have bargained away your soul to escape the trauma. But months or years later, you look back upon the experience, and it looks completely different. I have often said of some experience, "At the time I thought that was the worst thing that I could experience, but as it turned out it was one of the best things that has ever happened to me." You can trust God's will to be slanted towards your best interests.

Discovering God's Will

Once you know about God's will, how do you go

about discovering his plans for your life? I have counseled with some people who make this task more difficult than it really is. Discovering God's will for your life is simpler than you may think.

You can discover God's will by reading it. His will for you is not cataloged in heaven. It is written down, and you already have a copy. We call it the Bible. This book tells you how God wishes for you to behave. God inspired it so you would have a guide for every good thing he wants you to do (2 Tim. 3:15-17). The Bible records how God has related to people in the past, and since he doesn't change, it helps us to know how he relates to us now. Sometimes the Bible gives specific ways for you to act. At other times it gives you principles to guide your behavior. But, in any case, the Bible is God's will set to words.

You can discover God's will by doing it. This may sound like nonsense to you, but it is true nevertheless. Students frequently say to me, "I want to know God's will so I can do it!" That statement is going at it backwards. Jesus said that if we first do God's will then we will know it (John 7:17). This simply means that God never gives us the complete itinerary for our journey. He reveals his will to us inch by inch as we progress along the way.

The Great Smokey Mountains are visible from where I live. There is a highway that meanders over the mountains, joining Tennessee with North Carolina. And sometimes the fog is so thick on that highway that one can see only a few feet in front of his car. If you were at the base of the mountain on one of these foggy nights, how could you get over? You could sit in your car and wish as hard as you could that the fog would disappear and then you would be on your way. But sitting still in your car would not get you across the mountain. You could, however, start out slowly, following the white line in the road, and travel the few feet of clearance in front of the car. When you traveled that short distance, you would be able to see a few more feet. When you traveled that distance, you would see a bit further. Perhaps your progress would be slow, but at least by responding to what you could see, you could make it to the other side of the mountain.

God's will works the same way. If you will get out of your closet and start doing today what you already know God wants you to do—love your enemy, go the second mile, turn the other cheek, forgive seventy times seven, and the like—God will reveal his will for you as you need to know it. Walk the few feet of clearance in front of you. Then you will be able to see a bit further. But keep moving! You can know God's will only as you do it.

It's Up to You

Karen is a college sophomore who also happens to

be my next-door neighbor. She is as intelligent as she is attractive, and not long ago she taught me something about the chemical makeup of the world that has an application to our spiritual growth. She told me that carbon, which is one of the most common elements, has two basic allotropic forms and under certain conditions it can change into either graphite (black pencil lead) or diamond.

The story about carbon illustrates something that is also true about you. God has made you with infinite potential. You have inside you everything you need to become a real, fully-alive human being. You have all the potential for becoming the mature Christian God wants you to be. Whether you realize that potential or not—whether you become diamond or graphite—-is up to you. The ball is now in your court. You can actualize your potential by finding and following God's will for your life; it is your decision. God will guide you and help you, but basically the person you become from here on is up to you.

10

LEARNING TO KEEP YOUR EYES OPEN

AN ANCIENT JEWISH RABBI DESCRIBED a human being in this way: "In four respects man resembles the creatures above, and in four respects the creatures below. Like the animals he eats and drinks, propagates his species, relieves himself and dies. Like the ministering angels he stands erect, speaks, possesses intellect, and sees." [15]

The rabbi's last reference was not to physical sight, for the animals have that too. He was talking about insight. It amazes me how many people blunder through life with their eyes open, but see nothing, They are so preoccupied reliving old hurts, failures, and mistakes they are not alive to what is happening in the present. And all too frequently this happens in the spiritual realm as well There are those today who need to hear again Jesus' words of sorrow for those who have ears but do not hear and eyes but do not see.

I have participated in religious gatherings where individuals have been invited to share their experiences with Jesus. Inevitably, people who have been Christians for years stand and tell about their conversion. There is nothing wrong with that, but it always raises a question in my mind: "Have you experienced anything more recently?" Outside of church it would seem odd indeed. What would you begin to think of me if every time you greeted me with a "What's happening, man?" I responded by telling you about the day I was born?

Do you remember those anonymous disciples returning to Emmaus following Jesus' execution (Luke 24)? They journeyed all day with Jesus, not knowing it was Jesus, because they had their spiritual eyes closed. If you want to become a real, fully-alive Christian, you must learn to keep your eyes open on your journey. What new thing is God doing in your life? What new things are you learning about him?

Jesus promised that the Holy Spirit would teach us new things (John 14:26). For years I thought that promise referred to books, lectures, and academic research. I am certainly not against these. They are the tools of my trade as a religion professor. They are valuable and have their place in one's spiritual pilgrimage. Yet there is another dimension that has largely been neglected in spiritual growth— the personal dimension that exists between yourself and God.

As you grow older, both chronologically and spiritually, your needs will change. You will perceive reality differently. You will respond to life differently. Matters that are unimportant to you now will become vital for you tomorrow. And you will discover God working in some unexpected ways if you keep your spiritual eyes open. What you learn personally from your own experience with God will be as important for your growth and development as what you learn from others about him.

There have been several things I have learned from my acquaintance with Jesus in the past several years. These are not unique. Others have learned the same things. But these are important to me because they have come out of my own struggles in life instead of one of my textbooks.

Jesus Is for Losers

One of the most important lessons I have discovered recently is that Jesus is for losers. Our contemporary society celebrates the beautiful people. We have cheers for winners. We value persons who succeed. Have you noticed that there are no bowl games for losers? Our whole society is based on competition. And in such a society it is easy to think of the winners as always the good guys. I have heard my share of Christians who claim God has solved all their problems. They have no hurts, failures, blemishes, or fears. It's all victory in Jesus. I used to make those claims too, but inside I knew they weren't true.

The difficulty with our "beautiful people" culture is that most people feel left out. Most of the people you pass in the street feel bad about themselves. They hurt. They are insecure and have self-doubts. They are haunted by fears and guilt. Perhaps you are one of them. If so, there is some good news for you. Jesus loves losers. He remarked on one occasion to some of the first-place finishers in Jewish society: "I came not to call the righteous, but sinners" (Mark 2:17). When I realized several years ago that I was not as good as I appeared to be and that Jesus still loved me, I learned first hand that he is for losers. No matter who you are, or how you have lived, Jesus accepts you. He loves you even if you don't like yourself. I can't conceive of any news being better than that!

Beliefs More Than Gossip

I have also learned from my pilgrimage with Jesus that my beliefs must be more than gossip. The word gossip is defined as a "rumor of trivial nature." And that's exactly what my beliefs were as long as I learned them from a book.

I know now that they must grow out of experience.

For the most part, I think that beliefs must follow personal experience if they are to matter at all. A sincere belief is a verbalization of experience. If I say, "I believe God is love," what am I really saying? If my statement is genuine, I am saying, "I have experienced God in my own life and I have found him to be one who loves me." If I have not actually experienced God's love, if I have merely memorized the words from the Bible and repeat them, my statement is gossip.

If I say to you, "I believe God is just," what am I saying? If my statement is real I will be saying, "I have encountered God daily in my life and he has always acted fairly and done what he promised he would do." If I have not experienced him in that way, my belief is just gossip.

Beliefs are merely experiences put into verbal form. If your beliefs are to be more than gossip, more than rumors of a trivial nature, you must have actually experienced them in your own life. Only in that way do your beliefs become convictions. To be a real, fully-alive Christian, you must believe from the bottom of you heart as well as with the top of your head.

Silent Moments Are Important

When I was younger I valued only mountaintop

experiences with God. I wanted to be on a spiritual high all the time. I feared those times in the valley when God seemed far away and my interest in spiritual things was at low tide. Consequently, I ran away from those times by either denying them or by fabricating enthusiasm. I have since learned that the silent times can be times of growth.

The Bible teaches that God can be absent as well as present. Isaiah said, "Truly, thou art a God who hidest thyself" (45:15). Job cried out in despair, "Oh, that I knew where I might find him" (23:3). The Psalmist lamented, "My God, my God, why hast thou forsaken me?" (22:1). The writer of Proverbs quoted God as saying, "They will seek me diligently but will not find me" (1:28).

There are moments in life when God is silent. There are times when we cannot feel his presence. Sometimes God's absence is due to our own sin. We behave in a manner that makes us insensitive to his presence. Yet I am convinced that there are other times God is absent on purpose.

When I taught my children to ride their bicycles, I would put my hand on the rear fender and run along behind them to keep them from falling. That was hard on me, but necessary for them. There came a time, however, when I had to let go the fender and permit them to ride on their own ability. And I believe God does the same for us. The only way we can reach our full potential is for God to remove his hand from our fender. He is always close, always caring, always there to pick us up when we fall. But we can never grow up if God does everything for us. We can never mature if he solves all of our problems. God sometimes hides himself from us so we will grow up and learn to do some necessary things for ourselves.

When it seems that God doesn't respond to your prayers as quickly as you think he should, when he doesn't smooth out all the problems you lay on him rather than losing faith in him, maybe you ought to increase your faith. Learn from those moments when God is silent. Does his silence mean you are misbehaving and are not tuned in to his frequency? Or is the silence his way of teaching you to handle the problem yourself? In either instance, the moments of silence can be opportunities of growth if you've got your eyes and ears open.

Miracles Still Happen

Leslie is an attractive and talented young woman whom I have known for several years and who recently taught me again that miracles still happen. When I first met her, Leslie was a soprano in the church choir. She was active in church activities, married, and the mother of one son. On the surface, she was one of the beautiful people in our society. But inside it was another story altogether. Her marriage was on the rocks. She had personal problems she couldn't handle. And from there things went from bad to worse. The marriage ended in divorce. She tried counseling, but struck out. Her particular problem was described by the psychology text books as one from which there was very little hope she would ever recover. From counseling she turned to drugs and from drugs to witchcraft. Nothing seemed to work. In total desperation, she decided suicide was the only way out. The night she planned to take her own life she happened to turn on her television set. The program on at that time happened to be a late-night show produced by a Christian network. The show's host was speaking to "someone" in the television audience who might be contemplating suicide. He was saying that God could help salvage a life no matter how devastated it was. He also mentioned that viewers could call the telephone number that kept flashing on their screen if they needed help. As a last-ditch effort, Leslie called the number. A counselor spoke with her. The next day he and his wife drove to the city where Leslie lived and spent the afternoon with her. For the first time she opened her life fully to God. And from that moment life and hope started flowing back into her veins.

As the counselor left Leslie's house, he asked her where she got the number she dialed the night before. She responded that it was the number flashing on her television screen. Then she learned the truth. The counselor told Leslie that the number she called was not on the screen the previous night. She had dialed the unlisted number of his private office. A check with the counseling center used by the Christian network verified that the unlisted number had not been released to the television station. Where did the number come from? Was it one of God's miracles?

When Leslie telephoned me long distance to share her experience, she did not end her story there. After experiencing God's salvation for the first time, she and her son moved to another state. There the pieces of her life began to come together again. She discovered new ways to use her talents in ministering to others. She was able to begin coping with life. And she is now working through that personal problem for which the text books offered little hope.

I rejoiced with Leslie over the turnabout in her life, but for several days I couldn't get that telephone number incident out of my mind. Was it really a miracle? After several days of puzzling about that, I realized how myopic I had become. It really made no difference how Leslie got the number she dialed that night. The real miracle was that God took a desperate, lonely, hurting, and empty young woman and brought her from death to life. He did that for Leslie. He has done that for me. He did that for you. I really do believe in that kind of miracle. You may feel helpless sometimes, but because of Jesus you are certainly not hopeless.

Take My Hand

George Fox, the father of the Quakers, once said that "there is one, even Jesus Christ, who can speak to thy condition." There still is such a one and he is still able to speak to your situation. John Wesley said, "If your heart is as my heart, take my hand." I invite you to do the same. You have started your pilgrimage on the life road. Welcome to the journey. Let's join hands and walk along together with Jesus.

NOTES

1. Keith Miller, *The Becomers* (Waco, TX: Word Books, 1973).

2. Alexsandr I. Solzhenitsyn, *The Gulag Archipelago Three*, trans. Harry Willetts (New York: Harper & Row, 1976).

3. Frank Stagg, "A Whole Man Made Well" in *The Struggle for Meaning*, ed. William Powell Tuck (Valley Forge, PA: Judson Press, 1977).

4. Paul Tournier, *The Meaning of Gifts* (Atlanta: John Knox Press, 1976).

5. Eberhard Arnold, *Salt and Light* (Rifton, NY: Plough Publishing House, 1976).

6. Dietrich Bonhoeffer, *The Cost of Discipleship* (New York: The Macmillan Co., 1961).

7. Fritz Perls, "Four Lectures" in *Gestalt Therapy Now*, ed. John Faqau and Irma Lee Shepherd (New York: Harper & Row, 1971).

8. Albert Camus, *The Fall* (New York: Vintage Books, 1956).

9. Fritz Perls, "Four Lectures," *Gestalt Therapy Now*.

10. John W. Drakeford, *Integrity Therapy* (Nashville, Boatman Press, 1974).

11. Paul Tournier, *The Person Reborn* (New York: Harper & Row, 1966).

12. T.B. Maston and William M. Pinson, Jr., *Right or Wrong*, revised 14th ed. (Nashville, Boatman Press, 1971).

13. Karl Menninger et al., *The Vital Balance: The Life Process in Mental Health & Illness* (NewYork: Viking Press, 1967).

14.Victor E. Frankl, *Man's Search for Meaning: An Introduction to Logotherapy* (New York: Pocket Books, 1972).

15. A. Cohen, *Everyman's Talmud* (New York: Schocken Books, 1975).